Born to Break the Curse

The Story of
Peter Mason James

Born to Break the Curse

The Story of Peter Mason James

Deborah B. Judge

Copyright Information

Born to Break the Curse
The Story of Peter Mason James
By: Deborah B. Judge

©2018 Published and Copyright by:
Good News Fellowship Ministries

ISBN-13: 978-1-888081-41-1
ISBN-10: 1-888081-41-4

No part of this book may be reproduced or transmitted in any form or by any means, electronic or mechanical, including photocopying, recording, or by an information storage and retrieval system, without permission in writing from the Author.

Although generational curses are very real, this is a work of fiction. Any resemblance to actual persons, names or content, living or dead is purely coincidental. Please see Word From the Author for further information.

Unless otherwise indicated, all Scripture quotations are from the Authorized King James Version of the Bible.

To contact Deborah B. Judge, please email:
remanddebj@mail.com

Printed in the United States of America

Format and Cover Design by Lisa Buck
lisa.joy.buck@gmail.com

There is no fear in love; but perfect love casteth out fear: because fear hath torment. He that feareth is not made perfect in love. –1 John 4:18

Dedication

DEDICATED TO ALL OF THE BROTHERS AND SISTERS IN CHRIST JESUS WHO ARE INCARCERATED ALL OVER THIS WORLD. KEEP PRESSING FORWARD AND LET YOUR LIGHT SHINE BRIGHTLY.

And to Mr. Rick Schenker, who wrote: Moteke and took time out of his schedule to talk to me about getting started as a writer. I had no idea what to do or how to begin. Your kindness was so appreciated. I wanted to give you a copy when this was completed and thank you in person but God called you home before it was finished. THANK YOU FOR BLESSING ME.

Thank-You

FIRSTLY I HAVE TO THANK MY LORD FOR TRUSTING ME WITH THIS WORK. THIS IS IN YOUR CAPABLE HANDS TO TAKE AROUND THE WORLD AND PLACE IN THE LIVES OF THOSE WHO IT WILL HELP.

TO MY SISTER and BIGGEST cheerleader! I am grateful for the help you gave me on this project. You have always been there for me and I am so thankful that I get to call you sis. Thank you for encouraging me and for being a good example of Godliness. I love you to life!

TO MY PARENTS, all three of you: Mom, Bio-Dad, and Daddy who raised me: I wouldn't be here without you. MY LOVE FOR ALL OF YOU STRETCHES FROM HERE TO ETERNITY.

TO MRS SOPHIA LESHER: My main EDITOR IN CHIEF- the ORIGINATOR! Thank you so much for your talents and for your kindness to take on such a huge project the way you did. I learned so much from you.

TO MR. DAVID LESHER: My COMPU/TECHNO/GURU/GENIUS. You have crazy skills and have helped me for the last 24 years (Shhh, our age is showing). Thank you for always being there to help and teach.

TO MR. DENNIS HICKEY: I was so honored to have someone of your caliber help me with this project. From the bottom of my heart: THANK YOU!

Contents

The Story of Peter Mason James	1
A Message	3
Mi Familia	15
The Tables Turn	21
Obstacles	27
Honor Thy Father and Mother	39
Fathers, Provoke Not Your Children to Wrath	45
The Bottom Falls Out	51
Anger, Despair, Depression: Oh My!	59
The Iron Cage	63
Gabe	69
Dis-Appointments	83
I Surrender	91
New Beginnings	105
Who Am I?	115
My Mountain, Myself	121
Have You Considered My Servant?	131
T.G.I.M.	137
Plea Deal	145
It is Time	153
It is Finished	163
Closure	183
I Do and I Forgive	191
God Moves in Mysterious Ways	195
Grateful Heart	201
Word from the Author	203

The Story of Peter Mason James
In The Beginning

A group of men and women, that appear to be somewhere in their 30's, have assembled once again for their monthly get together, but this is no ordinary gathering. These young adults share a very dark bond with each other. They have come together for a sacrifice. Something, or someone, has shed its blood and they are eager for the taste. They stand together in the basement of their leader. The floor is marked with a pentagram and they all stand around it. Inside the pentagram appears to be a painted red "S" that looks as though it is dripping blood. The only light that can be seen is the flicker of candles. Each person is dressed in a long, black robe with the same red "S" encrusted over the heart of each robe that is seen inside the pentagram. They all wear hoods over their heads. There is an otherworldly darkness that engulfs them. The group chants as they pass a black cup around. Each takes a sip. As the blood of their sacrifice enters their mouths, their eyes dart around wildly, almost in a frenzy. This is not their first time indulging in this drink offering. Once the cup passes back to the leader of the group, the chant intensifies. As he drinks the last of the blood in this cup, he shrieks in an unnatural and frightening voice:

"All hail Satan."

The group follows the leader and they chant repeatedly:

"All hail Satan."

They have just made an offering to their master, the devil. Who are they?

A Message

Deuteronomy 5: 8-10

> *"Thou shalt not make thee any graven image, or any likeness of any thing that is in heaven above, or that is in the earth beneath, or that is in the waters beneath the earth: Thou shalt not bow down thyself unto them, nor serve them: for I the Lord thy God am a jealous God, visiting the iniquity of the fathers upon the children unto the third and fourth generation of them that hate me, And shewing mercy unto thousands of them that love me and keep my commandments."*

My name is Peter Mason James, "PJ" for short, and this is my story. My reason for writing this book is because God has molded my heart into one of help and concern for people struggling with things in their life. What things, you may ask? Well, let me explain where I am going with this.

There are so many repeated issues within families and most people don't understand that some of it can be linked to the supernatural. You see, there is such a thing as generational curses. You may not want to believe what I just said and that is surely your choice. I believe there are many people walking around wondering why they are the way that they are. Why do they behave the way that they do? Why do many people in their family behave the same way? Why can't they seem to break through into anything good in their lives? If you have been looking for an answer, you are who this book has been written for.

Let me give you an example of what I am talking about when I say "generational curse." I want you to look at patterns in your life and your family's life. Perhaps you struggle with alcoholism. Okay, now look at your family. You may clearly see that your mother and father also struggle with alcoholism. If you continue looking, you know that your grandfather on maybe your father's side also has a problem with booze. Your siblings are fighting this also. You can even track this to your children who go on binges of their own. It is highly likely that there is a generational curse loosed in your family.

I'll give you another example. You're divorced. Your parents are divorced. Your grandparents were divorced. All of your siblings are in and out of destructive relationships and none of them can stay married either. Or perhaps miscarriages run rampant in your family. Chances are, there is a generational curse loosed upon your family.

Right now you may be saying to yourself,

"Whoa! This is nuts."

Is it? Take a hard look at the evidence. There are patterns, destructive patterns, that you may see in yourself and your family right now as you read these words. There is no such thing as "good or bad luck." If you want to be free, you first have to be honest. That is why I am writing this book, and I am going to be very candid in telling my story.

Another question that you may ask is what is causing these curses? Well, to put it bluntly, at some point in a family's history a demonic door was opened and a debt was incurred to Satan that he is presently collecting on. Yes my friend, demons are real and so is Satan. It is foolish to believe in God but not believe in the devil. If that is you, you are guilty of only believing half of the Bible. It's even more foolish to say that none of this is real and it's all a joke. Are the tragedies that have happened to you or your family anything to laugh at? If Satan can maintain his deception, you are an easier target to allow him to enlarge hell. In John 8:32 Jesus says "And ye shall know the truth, and the truth shall make you free." It's truth time!

Some people reject the fact that there are demons active in the world and in their lives because by ignoring this truth, it makes it easier for them to ignore Christ. These are people that do not want to submit/surrender to God, so they reject everything. They deceive themselves into believing that they can be good without God and can control the evil in their lives. When Jesus died and rose from the dead, He rose with ALL power in His hands so if the One with the power over everything is not living in you, you have absolutely nothing in you that will fight the demonic strongholds in your life.

Even as I pen this, I have a hatred brewing in me. I hate the fact that so many people are shackled by the devil. I hate that each second hell is being enlarged by people. Did you know that hell was not created for us, but for Satan and the angels who followed him in rebellion against God? It is not a place where God desires you to be and NO, He doesn't send anyone there. A person sends him or herself to hell by rejecting Jesus Christ. You may not want to believe in heaven or hell but my friend, just because you don't believe doesn't make them any less real. My mission, through the Holy Spirit, is to snatch as many people out of Satan's hands as I can by speaking the truth of the Gospel of Jesus Christ!

Getting back to generational curses, many people get defensive when they are told that there may have been a demonic door opened in their life or that of their family. I hear so often, "But I don't worship the devil!" If you have never invited Jesus Christ into your heart and have never believed that God raised Him from the dead, there is only one god that you are serving: Satan. Even those who have given their lives to Jesus have to allow the Holy Spirit to clean house!

Psalm 51:5 says,

"Behold, I was shapen in iniquity; and in sin did my mother conceive me."

None of us were born saved. According to the Holy Scriptures, we were born in sin. The minute we enter this world, the devil is busy interrupting our lives. Why do I use the word "interrupt?" Because that is just what he does. He sends all kinds of temptations and people our way to keep us from Christ and our destiny in Him. One of my favorite points to tell people when I am speaking to groups is,

"If you like 'em tall, dark and handsome, Satan will not send you someone short, light and ugly."

He's a great strategist!

Previously, I said that those of us who are Christians have to allow the Holy Spirit to "clean house." Let me share some wisdom with you. The word SALVATION is a verb. It is an action word and because it is an action word, we can never stop allowing God to grow in us and through us. Sometimes that growth hurts but I would rather experience pain going through His process than be stuck repeating the same sin over and over again. We must daily, invite the Holy Spirit to show us what may be hiding in us.

Many of us have strongholds. This is something contrary to the Word of God that you are bound by that has a strong hold over you. Whether it is gambling, lust, pornography, lying, bitterness, jealousy, unforgiveness, these are just a few of the things that bind some Christians. People think that the minute they confess Jesus as their Savior that they will never have to work on themselves again. That is why so many people attending church every Sunday are saved but still bound. You can't ignore your process of spiritual growth and learning. James 1:14 says "But every man is tempted, when he is drawn away of his own lust, and enticed." Sounds to me that all of us need to know what our own lust is. If we are supposed to know the forces that try to lead us away from Christ, that must mean we need to know what makes us tick. Also, because we need to know our own lust, it is vital that as we go through deliverance, we ask God to show us what we need to do. Don't try to copy how someone else got free of a sin. God may take you on a completely different path. Don't be trapped by sin. Jesus died for you to be free INDEED!

Let us discuss the family unit. It is such a blessing for a child to be born to Godly parents. Our parents are supposed to be the earthly example to show us who our Heavenly Father is and how we are to relate to Him. When we grow up with parents that know Jesus and are truly saved, they should be living the Word in front of us and teaching us who we are in Christ. Sometimes this is resisted by the child as he or she grows and begins seeking their independence, because we have our own stubborn will. Look back at your life and think about the times your parents told you not to touch the stove because it was hot, but you just had to find out for yourself! That is your will going against the sound advice and stern warning from the authority and love of your parents.

There are people who grew up with parents who didn't believe in Jesus, couldn't have cared less about Him or even want His name mentioned in their presence and they have found Christ. If your parents were not Christians, that does not mean you cannot become a follower of Christ. Many children grew up in homes where the blessings of God were not spoken to them: however, our Heavenly Father has spoken plenty blessings for us to receive in His Word. (Glory to God!) Find your way to Him today and don't hesitate, for tomorrow is not promised.

People have said to me that Christians are a bunch of robots and have no choice in their lives. They use this as a justification to keep running away from their Creator. I love to be able to pull out my Bible to Genesis chapter 2 and 3. In Genesis chapter 2 verses 16-17, God tells Adam that he can eat freely of every tree in the garden EXCEPT the tree of the knowledge of good and evil, and says,

> *"For in the day that thou eatest thereof thou shalt surely die."*

Two things are important here, God told Adam what he couldn't eat of, and goes on to warn Adam of the consequences if he does. In chapter 3 of Genesis, you will find the serpent tempting Adam and Eve away from God. In this entire exchange, God never interrupts and forces His creation to obey Him. He leaves it up to Adam and Eve to either listen to Him or disobey. Unfortunately for them and us, they chose to disobey. Now if Christians were "robots," why didn't God force His will into this situation? All of us are given a choice. We can choose right or we can choose wrong.

As great a man as the Apostle Paul was, even he said in Romans 7:15-21,

> *"For that which I do I allow not: for what I would, that do I not; but what I hate, that do I.*

> *If then I do that which I would not, I consent unto the law that it is good. Now then it is no more I that do it, but sin that dwelleth in me. For I know that in me (that is, in my flesh,) dwelleth no good thing: for to will is present with me; but how to perform that which is good I find not. For the good that I would I do not: but the evil which I would not, that I do. Now if I do that I would not, it is no more I that do it, but sin that dwelleth in me. I find then a law, that, when I would do good, evil is present with me."*

Becoming a Christian does not make a person perfect. Once we accept Jesus as Savior, He brings His light but we can still struggle with sin. Paul wrote much of the New Testament but still had to fight against his weaknesses.

Furthermore, Matthew chapter 12 beginning at verse 43 says that,

> "When the unclean spirit is gone out of a man, he walketh through dry places, seeking rest, and findeth none. Then he saith, I will return into my house from whence I came out; and when he is come, he findeth it empty, swept, and garnished. Then goeth he, and taketh with himself seven other spirits more wicked than himself, and they enter in and dwell there: and the last state of that man is worse than the first. Even so shall it be also unto this wicked generation."

First and foremost, this is Jesus speaking in Matthew 12. He is teaching us how a Christian gets free and stays free from the strongholds of sin. The reason why I stress "Christian" is because if Jesus is not living in you, the devil is under no obligation to leave you. He is referring to demons. Christians cannot be possessed by demons but can be oppressed by them. So here you are, a Romans 10:9 Christian who has confessed Jesus Christ as your Lord and believe God raised Him from the dead, and you recognize a stronghold in your life. You want it gone and you command it to leave in the name of Jesus. This is only the first step. Jesus teaches us that this demon leaves and seeks another place where it can be satisfied. When it does not find suitable accommodations, it goes back to its house, which is you. It peeks in and sees that your house is absolutely empty, because you did not fill it with the Word of God. There is nothing that will keep it from coming back to torment you. Because you made it leave, it's thoroughly enraged. To make you pay it goes and gets seven more demon spirits worse than itself. The state you are in now is worse than before you made it leave.

Let me break this down a little further. If you are a drug addict and you confess Jesus as your Lord and Savior and believe God has raised Him from the dead, according to Romans 10:9, you are saved. You have become a Christian but you still crave drugs. You make the demon of addiction leave you in the name of Jesus and you stop there. You continue going to church, you join the choir, the usher board and drive the church van. All of those are good things, but the empty space that that demon once occupied hasn't been filled with anything that will keep it out, such as prayer, fasting, the Word and asking the Holy Spirit to now occupy the empty space. So now the demon comes back and sees this and brings seven demons worse than it is. Now, not only are you back on drugs but you are stealing from your loved ones. Not only are you stealing from your loved ones, you are robbing stores. You are prostituting yourself. You are taking money that would feed your children and feeding your addiction. When prostituting yourself isn't enough, you begin to prostitute your children. You are beating people up to take their money from them. You are running drugs for the dope man but taking your cut also to feed your addiction and placing yourself and your children in jeopardy.

Jesus is referring to this downward spiral. Things that you have never done before, you now do freely. Satan won't stop there. He's going to make you and everyone around you pay. You may pay with losing the trust of those who used to trust you. You may pay by losing your children, who you really do love, to foster care. You may pay by being locked up. You may even pay with your life. Additionally, drugs are just a symptom of something going on that you are trying to ease the pain of. Until that pain or rejection, abuse or abandonment is dealt with and you allow the Holy Spirit to heal you, you will constantly have a missing link in your protective fencing. That hurt, pain or whatever it is, is the keeper of the gate. That is what opens the gate to your soul for all the other demons to come in. Dear one, understand that whatever has happened to you in your life, Christ already defeated it on the Cross. You don't have to be afraid to let Him deal with it. Trust Him.

Now that God has your attention, let me share with you something that He has shared with me. As I stated, Salvation is an action word and the foundation of Christianity. This is a good and firm foundation. To become a Christian all you need to do is ask Jesus into your heart and believe that God has raised Him from the dead. Now, you are firmly in His hands. From there, we must evaluate ourselves and daily ask the Holy Spirit to reveal to us the things in us that are not pleasing to Him. Once this is done and you are truthfully ready to be free renounce anything not pleasing to God in the name of Jesus and immediately invite the Holy Spirit to occupy that area. This is what we call "deliverance." Think of it this way: you give the Holy Spirit permission to dig the sin out of you and remove it but then that area needs to be occupied by Him. How do you hold onto your deliverance? Look at John the 15th chapter. In Romans 10:9, we ask Jesus to come live in us, but John 15 tells us to abide/live in Him. This is how we hold onto our deliverance, stay free, and are able to walk in holiness.

Before I move on to my story, I want to give those of you who have never accepted Jesus Christ into your heart as your Savior and want to do so now, the opportunity. You do not have to perform anything, get right with God first or donate any money to any church. All God wants is you. Believe it or not, you are not reading this book by accident. God led you to it because it is your time for a new life through Christ. Just repeat this prayer after me:

> *"Lord Jesus, I confess that I am a sinner in need of Salvation. I invite You now into my heart to be my Savior and Lord. I believe that You died for me and that God raised You from the dead. Lord how I need You! Please wash me clean as I exchange my life, for Your life. I ask that You forgive me of my sins and Holy Spirit I invite You to lead me daily. Teach me to walk in You and live in You. By this confession I believe in faith that I am now saved. I am healed. I am delivered, and I am who the Bible says I am, in Jesus' name. Amen."*

If you prayed that prayer, Christ now lives in you. Please don't expect "super powers" or anything like that. Just understand that Jesus loves you and He lives in you now. It is also important that you find a church that is being led by a pastor who has a heart for God. Find a church that teaches the Word of God and where the leadership is living the Word of God. Don't expect perfection because none of us are perfect.

I also want to take time for those of you who are saved but have turned away from God and want to come back to Him. Please repeat this prayer:

> *"Lord God, I thank You for the opportunity to come back to You. I thank You that You did not allow me to die in my sin or in a backslidden state. I want to come*

A Message

home to You. I repent for trying to do things my way. I ask that You please forgive me and I place myself back into Your loving hands. Thank You, Lord, for saving me and bringing me back home. In Jesus' name I pray. Amen"

As I share my story with you, I want you to be able to look at your own life and your family. When I realized that we were bowing down to Satan, I understood then that was why so much destruction was in our home and our lives. For some of my story, as I reflect back, I will use my journal. Yes, I keep a journal in order to give you a more accurate account of the things that I experienced and the transformation that I owe to Christ. My journey starts off very dark and violently because, well, what happened to me and many of my friends was dark. It was probably the worst thing this little town had ever seen and it changed many lives. I am going to share my heart with you and as I do, I look forward to more of God's healing.

God bless you and walk with Jesus!

In His Service,

Peter

Mi Familia

I was born one hot summer day in June, many moons ago, to Frank and Katherine (or KayLynn as she was called) James. I was their first bundle of joy. You know, the one they would make all the mistakes with. Actually my parents were very good providers. My father, Frank was an Aerodynamics Engineer and because he was a specialist in his field he was able to move from place to place wherever he was needed. My dad took advantage of being able to move often, much to my dislike. I always hated being uprooted because I was never able to make friends but when you're a child you have to go along for the ride. My mom was a stay at home mom. I was thankful to have at least one of my parents around.

My parents seemed kind of an odd couple, at least to me. My dad was a very, very intelligent man, but not talkative. He stayed to himself for the most part and didn't seem to have many friends. My mother, on the other hand, could just light up a room. My mom was blessed with a smile that could melt the coldest of hearts. One day when I was older I got the nerve to ask her how she and my dad met. Throughout her story, I felt like I was on a rollercoaster. There were things that she disclosed to me that made my eyes almost bug right out of my head. It seemed almost like a cleansing for her to be able to sit down and share these things with her firstborn.

My mom was a beautiful curly-headed girl with high hopes of becoming a school teacher. She loved children and wanted to be able to teach the younger ones. Often the parents in her neighborhood would hire her to babysit because they knew if they could hire her their children were in for a stimulating journey filled with fun. She said that if she could help mold the mind of a child she could help him or her shoot for greatness.

Mom said she was a pretty good student and enjoyed classroom time, especially science and English. She was an honor student and very popular. Her parents pushed her in her education and made every resource available to her that she needed. Apparently, Grandma and Grandpa were old school churchgoers and ran a tight ship. She said that even though they were strict, she saw this as love and protection. They told her all the time that they wanted her to be able to have the things that they lacked. According to my mom, her parents' lives were not easy. Grandma Rosey, was a high school dropout and her dad was drafted into the military right out of high school. Grandpa Dan was on leave and had gone to a local nightclub with some of his sailor buddies. He met my grandma while listening to the sounds of jazz one summer night and they fell in love.

I had no idea that Grandma was actually pregnant before they had married. Sometimes when you see people later in life and they are so rooted in God and the church, you forget that they weren't born that way. I guess Grandma hid the fact that she was pregnant as long as she could but when she started to show a little her mother became suspicious and asked her outright. When it came out that she was, her dad kicked her out of the house and disowned her. She moved in temporarily with one of her cousins until Grandpa came to get her.

They were married at the local courthouse because they had no money for a wedding and, right away, Grandpa left again. My mom said that Grandma always told her that even though they were poor, having her was a joy. Her dad had only seen pictures of her for the first year of her life. Grandma told her that when he laid eyes on her for the first time, he was overwhelmed with love.

While Grandpa spent two more years of his life in the military he sent what little money he earned back home to his wife. She picked up hours at a neighborhood laundromat. Mom said that she remembers times when they didn't have much food but her mom always seemed to provide. When Grandpa was close to being discharged he came home with a surprise. He told Grandma that he was now a born-again Christian and wanted her to join him. Well, she wasn't so tuned into what he said to her because she had learned that while he was home on leave a few months back she had gotten pregnant again. She was afraid to tell him because they had no money for another mouth to feed. It was his reaction to her "upsetting news" that made her take notice of his new walk.

Mom said that Grandpa picked Grandma up and twirled her around shouting,

"Praise God! You have blessed us with another child and we will raise our children to know and honor You."

I guess Grandma was left speechless. Her reality was that there would soon be four mouths to feed with very little money. Her husbands' reality was that this was a blessing from God. He went on to tell her about what happened to him when he found his way to the Lord.

After Grandpa Dan left to go back to where he was stationed he wandered into a store to buy a can of soda. A guy came in to rob the store and seeing Grandpa's uniform took him as a threat. The robber attacked him with a knife, barely missing his vital organs. He never wrote Grandma to tell her because he didn't want to worry her. He had a letter drafted by one of his friends to deliver to her if something should happen. He remained in the hospital for a week and while he was there he was placed in a room with an older gentleman who happened to be a pastor. This pastor looked over at Grandpa and after introducing himself he said,

"Young man, if you were to die today, what would happen to you?"

Grandpa said he immediately got angry and told the man to mind his own business! This preacher said, "Son, you are my business. I was going about my daily routine, when all of a sudden I began to have chest pains. My secretary rushed me to this hospital. While on the way here, the good Lord said,

"I am sending you to speak to a young military man whose name is Dan."

Grandpa rolled his eyes at the man. He interrupted him and said,

"Excuse me but that is not hard information to find out."

He said the preacher continued and told him that if he gave his heart to the Lord, he would not have to worry about how he would support his wife, daughter and new baby because God already had a plan. Well, that got his attention. However, he told the man that he only had one child. The preacher said,

"God told me that your wife was with child."

They spent the next day discussing what Jesus had done on the Cross and how He had died and risen again for us all. Mom said when Grandpa told Grandma about this he began to cry. She had never seen him cry before except when he laid eyes on his daughter for the first time. Thus began their new adventure with God.

My uncle Christopher was born and according to my mom her parents were always blessed with jobs and were always able to take care of their family and bills. She said that they kept her and Uncle Christopher very close to them and made sure they were in church whenever the church doors were opened. They grew up thinking that this was the norm and that church was just a part of life.

She said her mom became an usher and her dad eventually became a deacon. Life for her and Christopher was school, church and then more church at home. Grandma and Grandpa were very loving but wanted them to understand that God was always to be an important part of their lives. Mom said that Christopher grew up, did so-so in school, and, as soon as he could, left and joined the military. He wasn't into the whole church scene. He rarely came home to visit because he knew if he did his Bible-thumping parents would force Jesus down his throat. Other than Christopher's frequent rebellion, her parents were the happiest couple she had ever seen in her life: that is, until she met my dad.

The Tables Turn

Mom met my dad, Frank, in the eleventh grade and was most taken with him. They had a couple of classes together, and she said she was always amazed at how he never seemed to pay any attention but whenever the teacher asked him a question, he could give the answer as though he were teaching the class. Dad was not a lazy student, just bored. Apparently, he excelled at everything he did but he missed quite a bit of school. According to Mom, he would just skip and said he had better things to do.

Although his presence in school was not consistent she said that he always turned his work in on time. His work was always exceptional, especially in science. This seemed to be the only class that really fascinated him, particularly when they had to dissect animals. Mom said she always hated that chore. Thankfully for her, they were paired up together on a number of science projects. She said he learned to dissect with such precision she just knew that with his smarts and his dissecting skills that he was headed to the medical profession.

She grew more and more fond of my dad and was especially drawn to his eyes. She saw such mystery in them that she would find herself staring deep into them while he was showing his skills on the unlucky frogs. She said that his eyes were a beautiful color but there were times when she looked deep into them and saw a strange darkness that intrigued her. Of course he noticed all of the attention she paid him and tried to play it cool with her. Finally one day, he asked her if she would like to meet him and some of his friends later. Mom said yes and knew that as strict as her parents were she would have to lie her way out of the house to see this boy to whom she had become so attached. She said she had never lied to her parents before but she had to see Frankie, as she called him, and she would do anything to meet him.

She told her parents that she was going to her friend Melissa's house to study for a test. Out the door she went. She ditched her book-bag behind a tree where no one would look and followed Frank's directions to a place he referred to as "The Spot." This was a secluded place where teen misfits hung out to pretend they were adults and drank and got high. She couldn't believe that she had never noticed this place and also couldn't believe how crazy some of the kids looked. She found it hard to believe that Frank would hang out here. Not because he wasn't weird in his own way, but because he was so intelligent. Most of these kids were messed up on drugs and booze. Everywhere she looked there were boys with long hair and earrings and girls with shaved heads. Everyone was passing joints. She felt very out of place but continued looking for Frank.

As she took in all of the sights and smells, she heard a familiar voice call to her from behind some junk cars that had been dumped there. She went over to him and before she knew it, everything seemed to disappear around her. It was now just her and Frankie. She had been so focused on school that she wondered if maybe love was tugging at her heart. There had been guys before, but never one that caught her in such a web.

Mom said that she found herself daydreaming about him all the time and doodling on her notebooks......MRS KAY-LYNN JAMES. In her words she couldn't shake him for anything. It made her gut ache wondering if he felt the same about her. She said he was always a hard read. He was never emotional about anything until one day.

At this point Mom stopped and looked at me.

She said,

"Peter, I'm going to share something with you that you cannot let your dad know I told you."

I gave her a look like,

"What in the world is my mother getting ready to say about her and my dad?"

I think she felt my fear.

"Relax," she said.

It was about my dad, not so much her. Just as soon as mom's eyes were spinning with this love talk about her early yearnings for my dad, her eyes dropped with concern.

She continued telling me how she wondered if Frank felt the same way about her. She was soon to find out. Frank was, in fact, smitten with her. Before she knew it, she was joining him in his dark world, bit by bit. She told me that about five weeks into their dating and sneaking around, he invited her to go to a secret place with him. He said it was a surprise and that he wanted to share something special to him with her. She said that made her heart thump. Here she was, walking hand in hand with the guy she knew she wanted to marry and he was taking her someplace special.

They walked in the direction of the teen hangout but kept walking past everyone. They followed some railroad tracks for about a mile, and went through an abandoned junkyard. He then led her into a wooded area. She stopped because she thought he was expecting something inappropriate from her. He said that he just wanted to show her something. Apparently my dad was usually a gentleman, although he had his moments.

They went deeper into the woods. She smelled something rancid in the air. They walked about another fifty yards and there it was. She would look upon something that would forever change her life. Frank opened his arms wide and told her to behold his artwork, "The Tree of Death!" She realized where the odor was coming from. Hanging from this tree were animals that Dad had apparently caught, skinned and or gutted. There were cats, small dogs, raccoons, rabbits and even birds. He had them hanging like they were Christmas ornaments!

Mom said she could not believe what she was looking at. These animals were in different stages of decomposition and she turned away and began to throw up. I could not believe what I had just heard. I think my mouth was hanging open. I had only known my father to be a suit-and-tie kind of a guy and it was a terrible shock to hear about this insane behavior from his teen years.

She continued telling me that when she looked up at him he looked like something else. I stopped her there and asked,

"You mean, someone else, right?"

She looked at me and said,

"Peter, what I saw in your father that day was not of this world. I thought I was hallucinating from being so sick. There was a darkness in his eyes. His entire being looked different."

I pressed her,

"What do you mean, different?"

She said,

"I can't put it into words. He seemed to disappear, momentarily and was consumed by something else. I couldn't move because I was so scared. Then suddenly, I was looking at the handsome man that I followed to his secret getaway."

She got up at that point and got a glass of water, clearly needing to collect herself. I needed a little time myself to let what she had just told me sink in. Firstly, why didn't she run and never give Dad a second thought? Then again, if she had, I wouldn't be alive today to tell you my story. The other question I asked myself was whether the horror that Mom saw that day had somehow come into me when I was born.

Mom came back and told me that although she was scared of what she thought she saw, she was still drawn to my father. She thought he needed help and she could provide it. She asked him why he had done this to those animals. His response was, "This is my art and my passion. Kay, everything that is born will eventually die and death is something that we should not fear. No one cared about these animals, but I do, and that is why I honor them this way."

She told him that she didn't want to see any more of his "art" so they walked back to the teen hangout. To try to get the thought of those poor animals out of her mind she smoked a joint and drank some booze. Frank came over and put his arm around her and kissed her on the cheek. She thought that what he did for entertainment was horrible but she still wanted him. Mom told me that for a while she had terrible nightmares about the creature she thought she saw in my dad. She would drink to make her fear go away: nevertheless, they were soon inseparable and she was helplessly in love with him. She said he never again showed her anything like what he had done to those animals. But then there was a new complication in their relationship: their parents.

Obstacles

My parents were now three months into their "secret" relationship. I guess the only ones that did not know about it were my moms' parents. She had met Dad's parents and they scared her. The rumor all over town was that they were Satanists, but Mom, being the naïve girl that she was, didn't believe it. She only knew that they could be downright abusive to Dad and they drank for breakfast, lunch and dinner. Dad's mom, Maria, was a ghostly-looking woman with jet black, greasy hair who cussed like a sailor. Mom told me that she had also gone to jail a time or two for stabbing my grandfather Johnny.

"As for Johnny, he was rarely ever seen coming out of the house other than to go hunting," she told me.

"He was a mean drunk and had a horrible habit of pointing his hunting rifles at anyone brave enough to come to the house. He liked to use fear as his weapon and your dad pretty much only went home long enough to change his clothes and eat. It was always so hard for me to believe that as attractive and intelligent as your dad was, that he had come out of that union."

She went on,

"One day we stopped by the house after giving my parents the slip. Johnny actually asked me who my parents were. In the few times that I had gone over there, if I saw him, he never said more than a grunt to acknowledge my presence. I told him that my parents were Christians, although I no longer followed religion other than when I was forced to go to church with them. That answer changed everything. He kind of seemed to embrace me more, and told me how much he hated Christianity."

Johnny told her that she was smart not to accept a God that didn't exist. Mom said that listening to him made her feel uneasy because her parents talked about God like He was sitting right there in the house with them. Johnny showed her a book that he said was his savior. He said it was The Satanic Bible and he cradled it in his arms like a newborn baby. She said that she began to understand some of the symbols in their house such as inverted crosses, pentagrams, Baphomet statues, 666 signs and black candles.

"One day, I hope my son will follow in my footsteps," he told her.

More and more, my grandparents saw Mom leaving church and leaving them. She began to be rebellious and reports were coming back to them about her drinking and smoking marijuana. They tried to talk to her, but it usually turned into shouting matches with Mom fleeing the house. My grandparents tried to have faith that God would dissolve this relationship, but Mom's choice was the love of her life. They felt there was little else they could do.

My dad's parents seemed to be more accepting of this union. They only accepted this relationship because they knew that my mom's parents rejected it. Talk about a brutal wedding! All of the pictures I've seen from the wedding are like this: on one side frowns and concern, and on the other side looks that seemed to say,

"Take that, suckers!"

No matter what happened, mom's parents continued their involvement with the church. I can remember sitting on my grandfather's knee as he cradled me in his arms. There was a favorite chair of his on the front porch of their house and all the neighbors seemed to swarm to their home every Sunday after church. Whenever we went for a visit, Grandpa would be full of stories from the "good ole days" and all the menfolk would join in with their round of "amens." Grandma was always busy in the kitchen making homemade lemonade. The smell of apple pies filled the air. I always enjoyed going to visit them until it was time to go to church.

The rule of the house was, if you stay here, you go to church on Sunday. As a result, my dad rarely ever went with us when we visited. Church was more than I could handle. I mean, how many kids do you know, that can sit still and FOCUS on some guy in a fancy robe talking endlessly? Mom would get so mad at me because I was into everything. I spoke out loud, I pulled on some of the women's wigs and did a lot of yawning with my outside voice. The only thing that would sometimes get my attention was the Cross that hung behind the boring guy talking. I rarely ever heard him mention anything about what it meant or what it was there for, but it drew me.

During one of our trips to church I did something quite embarrassing. Mom said that she expected me to stay awake during the services because I was older. My little brother Brian was always allowed to curl up on her lap and go to sleep. The boredom I felt whenever we were in this place was overwhelming. I always remember the constant, stand up, sit down and the endless sermons on how God expects you to give your money. I'm telling you, people would put so much money in those trays when they were passed around that you could've sworn they were trying to buy their way into heaven. So this particular Sunday I guess I just felt the need to force my little brother to sit through the torture along with me. Right at a very quiet part of the service, I yelled, "Hey Brian, wake up!" Brian, who was sleeping like a little angel, was jarred awake and began screaming. Everyone turned and looked at my mom like they were burning holes through her. I thought it was great! Grandma and Grandpa didn't make us go to church anymore when we visited.

When my mom announced that she was pregnant with my brother Brian it prompted a time of mixed emotions for my parents. They were happy another child was coming and I'd have company, but also concerned that the new bundle of joy would be like me. I would hear them saying things like, "I sure hope this baby is peaceful" or "Hopefully this baby won't behave like Peter." Whenever I heard them talk like this it hurt. I felt like I was a bad child. As young as I was, I hoped that this child didn't have to go through what I was going through.

When my mom went into labor, I hoped real hard for a little brother, and that is exactly what I got. Brian Allen James came calmly into the world shortly after Christmas. When I was finally allowed to visit, Mom was holding little Brian in her arms. I climbed up on her bed and looked at the new addition to the family. I said to Mom,

"He's funny lookin'."

The second thing out of my mouth was,

"Please sleep good."

And he did.

Months went by, and Brian seemed like my complete opposite. He was an easy, happy baby. Most importantly, he rested well. I remember how I would watch him at night because I couldn't sleep. He was such a good boy and I loved him so much. As for me, I suffered with tormenting nightmares. My dad stayed busy at work while mom raised two children virtually alone. I needed my dad so much but, as usual, he wasn't there.

My mom told me that from the day I was born I was screaming. She said she would spend hours burping me, bouncing me, walking me and making silly faces at me, but nothing worked. This took its toll on my mom because she had very little help from my dad. His work ended when he left his office so if he had to work until midnight, that's what he did.

She said I was a pretty good child apart from crying a lot and not sleeping much. It wasn't that I refused to sleep, it was that I couldn't stay asleep. She said that I would drift off, exhausted from screaming, just to wake up screaming all over again. She and my dad had their suspicions about what was happening but they didn't know how to help me.

I told her,

"It must be hard on a parent to stand by and see their child going through something and not know how to help. Babies can't just tell you to change their diaper, or they want to be held or that there is something frightening happening to them when they sleep."

Mom said,

"As time went on, your night fits became worse and sometimes even violent. I would even put you in bed with me at times hoping it would give you peace, but whatever you were struggling with in your sleep just didn't care."

I remember trying to wake from my sleep, and I would be physically swinging. When I opened my eyes, I was fighting my mom or dad. They knew something was wrong with their son.

As I got older, my parents knew they could not put me in daycare or preschool. Mom could have used a break so that she could get some rest. They wouldn't even leave me with babysitters very often because of the "strange" outbursts I would have. One time they took a chance and got a sitter. She was a young woman in her early 20's who lived three houses down from us. I was somewhere in my toddler stage. My parents just wanted to leave me with her so they could do some Christmas shopping. I guess I put quite a fear in this poor lady because Mom said she got a frantic phone call from her. The sitter told her that after feeding me and playing with me some, I drifted off to sleep. Mom said her gut just dropped at hearing this. The sitter put me in my crib and less than an hour later, she heard unimaginable screams from my room. She ran to see what was wrong and saw something that frightened her to her core. My crib was being shaken by some unseen force to the point where it was literally coming off the floor. My arms and legs were flailing about wildly as though I were fighting something.

The babysitter called for her roommate to come over and help her. It happened that her roommate was a Christian. She began to read the ninety- first Psalm. The sitter told my mom that her roommate uttered a prayer and commanded this evil to stop in the name of Jesus Christ. The crib immediately stopped shaking and I woke up. Although I was awake, I was still fearful and crying. My mom and dad rushed home to find the sitter crying herself, wearing her coat and ready to leave. Her roommate had left just before they got there. As you can imagine, this young lady never ventured back to our house.

Mom and Dad started taking me to doctors and psychiatrists when I was around six. Apparently, I was old enough to explain to them that I was seeing monsters in my sleep and in my room and they were the ones trying to hurt me. This sounded unreal to them. They thought I was experiencing sleep deprivation psychosis at six years old. I was taken to every kind of doctor you could imagine. The MD's and Psychiatrists both diagnosed me as being Schizophrenic. I was given medications, but nothing stopped the torment.

Since I have been telling my story, people are always very interested in details about these beings. I don't know if it is because they really are interested or just trying to see if I'm making them up. Imagine the darkest of shadows, but with substance. To me as a little boy, they looked like giants. Most of them were huge but even the smaller ones were extremely violent. They had a supernatural strength. One of the most frightening things for me was that most of the time, during these terrors, I would be standing in total darkness, afraid to move forward or even sit down. From out of nowhere these monsters would appear and attack.

The fear that I felt growing up is indescribable. When I did get a look at them, their faces were distorted. Their eyes were intense red and filled with hatred. Some looked almost animal-like. Think of the scariest horror flick you have ever watched in your life that contained beings that made your skin crawl. Multiply that by a thousand and you'd be close to looking at my unwelcome night visitors. Their smell was something that has always stayed with me. Combine all the garbage dumps in the state, mix it with rotten eggs and throw in decaying flesh, and the smell of sulfur, that's what they breathed on me. It was unbearable.

They did all kinds of unimaginable things to me in my sleep. When I think back on this, I keep referring to sleep but their torment felt completely real. The violence inflicted on me seemed to bring these creatures an evil joy. I could hear them communicate with each other, but could not understand what they were saying. Their voices sounded very garbled. When I heard them shriek and scream it felt like they were telling each other of new plots to attack me. I would sometimes wake up with severe scratches up and down my arms, legs or even my back. Many times my parents would find me coming out of one of these fits with bruises around my throat as though I had been choked. It seemed that something was trying to kill me in my sleep, but it (or they) enjoyed the torture more. I would jump up gasping for breath. My parents would come running. As I write this, please understand that reliving this is not easy for me. I know that this must be part of this book because it is part of my story and somewhere, someone will read this that knows exactly how I feel because it is their story too.

It wasn't until I became a Christian that I realized that the beings I referred to as "monsters" were demons. I learned that from the time we are born, demons study us and it is their job to keep us from coming to Christ and walking in our destiny. They play for keeps because they know that once we open the door of our heart and invite Christ into it, not only do they lose us, but we become a threat to them.

There is nothing nice or pleasant about them. Oh, often they try to wrap the package up nicely, but none of it is real. The package may come in the form of money, beautiful women, men who promise you everything you want to hear, or influence. They can deceive you into feeling that you are more important than God but when they are done with you, they drop you like you are nothing. If you find yourself desperate for fame and will do anything to make it, all the wrong doors will open to you, and they will want your soul in return. They use you for a season and, for those foolish enough to reject Christ, your soul is theirs for eternity. For a time it has the appearance that it is wonderful because the Bible says in 2 Corinthians 11:14,

> *"And no marvel; for Satan himself is transformed into an angel of light."*

When they show what they really are and your life falls apart many times it is too late.

My most obvious problem was fear. This demonic spirit had a tight hold on me. My parents had no idea how to end any of this and watched me live a life on the edge. I guess the devil thought that if he could keep me scared all the time that I would never find my way to Christ. He was wrong!

Satan uses fear, more specifically, fear of the supernatural. After becoming a Christian and being delivered from the spirit of fear, I have been blessed to be able to minister to countless children who have shared with me about unholy visitations in their rooms in the middle of the night. Much like me, these children go to their rooms, which should be a place of peace, and it is soon transformed into more of a haunted house packed with the terrors of hell. Sleep becomes difficult (to say the least) because of the fear. What an invasion it is for a demonic spirit to step from the supernatural into the natural world and into our home at will. Parents, if you have children telling you that there are things scaring them in their room at night, please LISTEN! Don't tell them there is nothing there, or that it's all in their imagination. They are there and they are not "pretend."

Not all the time that I spent asleep involved violence from another dimension or world. When I got older, there were two recurring dreams I had. I didn't understand what they meant but they always stayed on my mind. In one of the dreams I vividly remember seeing these people dressed in black robes. They were always standing in a circle around a pentagram that was painted on the floor. They'd be chanting something that sounded so wicked. I would always try to shake myself out of this dream but to no avail. They were saying something about Satan in their chant and passing a large cup around with something red in it. It always ended with the one who appeared to be the leader taking the last drink and holding the cup up as the chant grew louder and louder. This dream would make me wake up in a cold sweat.

The other dream was the one wherein I felt the most peace. I would be standing in a bedroom. Everything about this room seemed very old. The furniture looked antique and the wallpaper on the walls was something that I have never seen in any store. It felt as though I had traveled back in time. There was always this little old lady kneeling beside her bed with her hands folded as though she were praying. She was so slender it seemed as though if you hugged her too tight, she would break. She always had the same ordinary gray dress on that buttoned up the front and a string of pearls hanging gently from her wrinkled neck. She had beautiful white hair that was always neatly pulled back into a bun. Every crease in her face gave her the appearance that she had lived a full life. The intent look on her face made me feel as though she was reaching out to a force that she knew was bigger than her. I could see her lips move but could never hear her speak. The sun was dazzling as it shone down on her as if to wrap itself around her.

Her bedspread was a pale pink and white with bursts of purple here and there and looked as though it had been carefully knit together. Sitting on top of her bed next to her was a beautiful worn Bible. From time to time, she would unfold her hands and place them ever so lovingly on it. She would open her eyes and I could see the dim traces of time in them. At times she'd clutch this Bible to her chest, close her eyes and seemed to pray all over again. I would always look around the room, feeling drawn to something. Just then I would feel this gentle breeze blow through her window. As the breeze blew, I could hear pages turning. The wind was blowing pages of a book filled with black and white pictures. I would walk over to look in amazement as each page turned slowly before me.

These must be the memories of her life being flashed before my eyes but I never understood why. I could see every person clearly, except the face at the end of the book, even though when I woke up I could not remember any of the faces. What I could remember is that the last picture seemed to be in color but as hard as I tried to make out the face, I couldn't.

The only thing I could tell is that it was a man. I would look back at her and then wake up. Who was the woman and why was she always invading my dreams? Why couldn't I hear her? Who was she praying for and who were the people in the photograph book?

Honor Thy Father and Mother

When I reached my teens, I began to strongly rebel against my parents. They didn't understand me and I didn't understand myself. There was so much going on inside me that I felt like I was going to explode. At times, I would hear voices tell me things like,

"If you steal out of your moms' purse, we'll leave you alone."

I would do what they said, thinking it would please these monsters and I would have a peaceful rest. They lied every time and all it would do was get me in trouble. I would try to explain to my mom and dad that "they" told me to commit whatever crime against them that I committed and their response was,

"You are using this as an excuse to do bad things but you were raised better than that."

It made me angry that they never believed me so I got worse. I would act out in school and cause all kinds of trouble for my teachers. Many times I was sent home for fighting. I was labeled a troublemaker and eventually put in an alternative school. This went over well with my fancy dad. Wherever we moved, I was in trouble and becoming more destructive. Truth is, I just didn't care anymore. I had a mom who never believed me because she thought this behavior was something I should have grown out of and I had a dad who was absent. My mom cried often and my dad, well, all he knew how to do was work his troubles away.

All I wanted to be was normal. My opinion of "normal" meant, peace in my mind, never moving again and having both my parents around me. I really felt like, if I was only born to be tortured, what's the point of my life? Boy, was that a thought dropped into my mind by these demons. I would often drink myself into a stupor and when that didn't help I would score some dope. I wanted this over. I was drifting away from life.

I was so troubled that my every thought was about death. I would think how nice it would be to not exist anymore. I could get plenty of rest then because I would just cease to live. I learned that this was another lie from the depths of hell but didn't learn it until years later. My family didn't believe in anything. Once I stumbled upon some weird items in our storage area but I didn't think they were anything relevant. After all, they were inside an unmarked box that was covered in dust. I think the only time it saw the light of day was when we moved. Inside the box were some black candles (that I never saw burn), some weird looking statues, and this really old book. The writing was very worn on it but it said something like "The Satanic Bible." My parents weren't Satanists! This must be stuff they had collected over the years for fun. I did notice a necklace my dad wore and asked him what the emblem was hanging from it. It looked familiar, like I had seen it somewhere before. He said it was a pentagram that had been passed down through his family and was about the only nice thing his father ever gave him.

I was able to dismiss this dust-covered box and life went on. I was still the sad, awkward teenage boy who continued to get into trouble. When I was sixteen, it no longer became a question of how I could make the misery stop, but when. I was at my end. The drugs didn't do it, the alcohol wasn't enough. I wanted out, and soon. People who have peaceful sleep and a nice life don't understand what it is like to be so afraid to fall asleep that you do anything to stay awake but I knew that if I drifted off "they" were coming.

One day, the tough boy at my school approached me. I thought he was coming to start trouble but instead he invited me to a party. I snuck out of the house in the middle of the night and headed there. This was a known party house but I had never been invited before. One of the kids there was showing off a gun he bought from a drug dealer and it piqued my interest. Maybe this was my way out. I inquired about how to get one and he told me that he would sell me that one for twenty bucks. I reached into my pocket and we made the illegal transaction.

I carried this gun around with me for weeks, keeping it out of my family's sight. After waking up one more time from a frightful night terror the urge to end my life was overwhelming. I decided that this is it, I can't take it anymore. I felt almost like my tormentors were pushing me forward, filling my head with thoughts like,

"This is the only way to stop us."

I looked in on my brother and cried knowing I wouldn't see him again and then scribbled a short note to my parents that said,

"I'm sorry and I love you."

I grabbed my gun and walked to the woods that surrounded our home. I hated the thought of my little brother or my mom finding me so I walked deep into the darkness that seemed so familiar to me.

I sat down and rested against a tree. I wanted the commotion in my mind and the violence in my sleep to stop. I loaded the gun with two bullets just in case the first one didn't do the job. My tormentors seemed to be right there with me telling me, "do it, do it now!" I lifted the gun to my head, sweat pouring down my face and put my finger on the trigger. Just as I went to pull the trigger, I heard this voice that sounded like many rushing waters say loudly to me: "PEACE, BE STILL!" I instantly dropped the gun and the voices stopped. I looked around but no one was there. Whose voice was that and why did I, for the first time in my life, feel peace? I later found out that those words are written in Mark 4:39 and they are written in red.

"Peace, be still."

Jesus was speaking!

I will never forget the day that I read that Scripture. Here was Jesus in the bottom side of a boat sleeping and His disciples were up top facing a great storm. Fear overtook them and I guess they forgot who they had as a passenger sailing along. Just when it seemed like the end was near and they would lose their lives, one of them had enough sense to call on Jesus who commanded the atmosphere! He literally made the storm stop.

That's what He did for me that night in the woods. He made the storm stop but in my ignorance, I didn't know then that it was Him. Could Jesus have been keeping me safe from death even in my unsaved state? Remember I said that we all have a destiny to fulfill and that it is the devil's job to keep us from it. The awesome thing, though, is it is the work of the Holy Spirit to lead us to it and He doesn't lose! Although my life was spared that night, I would soon face another battle.

I thank God that He intervened for me that night. He didn't let me take my life, especially in the disturbed state that I was in. It really is true what the Bible says in John 10:10:

"The thief cometh not, but for to steal, and to kill, and to destroy: I am come that they might have life, and that they might have it more abundantly."

The thief, being Satan, comes to steal from us and our families. He will take anything that is precious to us. He comes to kill our marriages, finances, and eventually he'll take our lives. He is a master at destroying. Look at the many families that have been torn apart by divorce. Look at how violent our schools have become since prayer has been taken out of them.

I remember the dreadful day of 9/11 and the lives that were stolen and the sorrow and terror that was unleashed on this nation. I said to God, "There has to be something in the Bible to show us what this attack was in the supernatural."

He led me to Revelation (get this) 9:11 which says:

"And they had a king over them, which is the angel of the bottomless pit, whose name in the Hebrew tongue is Abaddon, but in the Greek tongue hath his name Apollyon."

Both of these names mean Destroyer or Destruction!

As I said, my life was spared that night in the woods but Satan, the destroyer, wasn't quite finished with me.

Fathers, Provoke Not Your Children to Wrath

An important issue is the role of parents, especially fathers, being in the home AND taking an active part in raising our children. Satan is very slick in his efforts to remove men from the home. He knows that men are the spiritual leaders and there is a certain authority that we carry. He has understood that if he could remove the man from the home, he can assault the family, but when a Godly man takes charge of his home and aligns himself with the Word of God, Satan doesn't stand much of a chance! Fathers can be removed in many ways from their homes. They can be absent fathers. They can be out of place fathers and by this I mean, the wife is in charge. Or they can be fathers that live in the house but are out of touch with their children. My dad was in the house but emotionally unavailable to us.

My father spent long hours working and when he was home he needed his rest. Needless to say, we didn't form much of a bond. My dad was always very distant from everyone. He never appeared to be satisfied even with everything he had accomplished in his life. There was a void in my dad that affected every member of the household. He never had time to do that "father-son stuff" with me because he always had deadlines or meetings that were more important. There were so many times I wondered if my dad even loved me or wanted me around because he just wasn't there for me.

I don't mean to sound like I didn't appreciate what my father did for me financially, but a boy needs more than material things from his dad. I learned the value of hard work but I also wanted to know the satisfaction of being taken up into my father's arms and told how proud he was of me. There are certain things that a father needs to pass onto his son but for some reason my dad seemed to not be able to commit. There was something keeping him from reaching out to me like a father should but, being just a boy, I didn't understand. All I knew is that whenever I was in a school long enough to play sports I'd look up in the stands and there would be my mom, not my dad. I saw the heartbreak in her because she knew this hurt me.

On so many occasions I would hear my mom and dad arguing about how he was never around. It always ended with my dad saying something like,

"Well I guess I'll just quit my job and stay home."

Often it would leave my mom sobbing. I knew he loved us, I wanted him to show us, but it seemed like he didn't know how.

The older I became, the more I understood that my dad hadn't received affection from his father either. This passed from one generation to the next. I began realizing that we weren't moving from place to place because he was being sent, we were moving around because my father was always requesting to be transferred. He would finish a job at one facility and then go on to the next. What was he running from? I would come to find out after many events unfolded in my family.

As a boy, deep in my heart, I knew that my father loved me but I wondered, would it hurt for him to show it? Sometimes I felt like, I wouldn't be tortured like this if my dad were here. We all have images of our father being like Superman, able to battle evil. I wanted my Superman there for me, keeping me safe, but he wasn't. It was always "work, work, work."

I became very bitter towards my dad as I got older. I hated moving around the way that we did. When I was old enough to realize that this was his doing, I was even angrier. Every now and again I would lash out at him and say things like,

"If we would stay put sometimes, maybe I could make some friends."

We sometimes fought something fierce. No matter how much I protested about the next move I was ignored.

All this moving around made me shy. Then there was the fact that I was always scared out of my mind by my tormentors in my sleep. I could never stay at a buddy's house or they stay overnight at mine. My secret had to be kept within the boundaries of our little house of horrors. My parents said they wouldn't let me stay overnight anywhere because they were protecting me. My father said one time that he would be too embarrassed if I "acted out" in my sleep at someone else's house. I can't even describe how much that hurt me.

The angrier I became towards my tormentors and my father, the more I acted out. I began to depend on drugs to escape the pain I felt. I hated life. I remember one day I was sent home from school after being in another fight. My dad was at home for some reason. He looked at me with great pain in his eyes. He saw his son slipping away from him but at this point, how could he start to be a father? He lowered his head and walked away. When I saw this, I tried to pull it together. He said something to me that day without saying a word. I was old enough to understand what pain and desperation looks like, and it was him.

As I write this, please understand that I am sharing with you how I used to feel toward my dad. I have since been healed by the power of God and God has shown me many things. I can take each memory of my childhood now and understand why my father was how he was. I thank the Lord that we are now able to spend time with each other and I was able to release him from all of the guilt he carried.

Life took a horrible turn when we made our last move. We moved to a small town just off the road to nowhere. This place was so rural that it seemed like everyone who drove vehicles prided themselves on trying to outdo one another with the fanciest tractor. In every direction all you could see were woods, fields, and cows. I hated it at first but after about four months I finally managed to make some friends, Jimmy, who had just left for college, Tony, Sam, and one who was referred to as "Tank."

Tank was every bit the town hero. He had the looks, the fancy car and the build to live up to his nickname. He was fun to be around but he could sometimes get out of hand. There were times that his personality would turn and he would go into rages. He was built like a machine and had definitely earned the respect of the other kids in the community. Rumor had it that he used steroids. He graduated from high school a year behind me and was the top athlete at school. He was popular with most everyone in town, especially the girls. Hanging around with him I was never short on "female companionship."

We were just fun-loving kids. From time to time I would let my little brother Brian hang out with us. Our favorite pastime was playing football in a field that was out of the way. We could make all of the noise we wanted there, run as hard as any

NFL player and then throw back some beers that Sam or I had swiped from our parents. When we finished playing football, showing off if any girls were watching, Tank would crank the stereo in his car and we would stay there late into the night.

I would say that out of all the guys, Tony was my best friend. When we graduated from high school, he got me a job at a local hardware store and we worked as hard as we played. I felt as though I was heading in a good direction. Mom was proud of me for having a job and Dad seemed rather pleased too. My boss was a great guy named Sal. He was in his late seventies, down to earth, and seemed to have a heart for young people. He would take a lot of time out of his day showing Tony and I how to fix things up. He knew so much and I enjoyed listening to his war stories. He was so open and would answer any questions that we had.

One day, I decided to pour out my heart to him and tell him about my relationship with my dad. They were so different. He just sat and listened to me as I fought back tears. For the first time ever, I realized how much it hurt to be so distant from my father, although we lived under the same roof. I knew in my heart that I really loved my dad. The problem was that I didn't know how to reach out to him because our relationship had grown so strained. When I finished talking, he said to me,

"Sometimes we don't realize that our parents carry wounds in their hearts that may stem from their childhood and, because of that, they can't relate to their own children. It's not that your dad doesn't love you, but it may be that he wasn't loved very much by his father so he has a hard time showing you affection. Peter, when the time is right, healing will happen inside both of you and then your relationship will be healed also."

I rested in those words.

I began to notice a change in my attitude toward my dad. I really loved this man and one day, while I was on my way out the front door to go to work, I told him how proud I was of all of his accomplishments. He looked at me over his glasses and with an uneasiness said,

"Thank you son."

To hear him say that one word, "son" took so much anger out of me. This was a huge step for us. Unfortunately, that happiness was short lived.

The Bottom Falls Out

One Saturday evening, me and the guys decided to reward ourselves with a game of football over at the field. My brother Brian was excited because I told him he could come along. I had a job and he was still in school so we didn't get to do much bonding. Brian went to suit up and I told him I'd meet him at the field after I went to the bank to cash my check. I walked to the bank, as everything in town was a stone's throw away from everything else. I talked a few minutes with the teller, Mrs. Wheeler, who invited me to come to her home to pick the apples off her apple tree. She said she had promised my mom that she would save some for her. We said our goodbyes and I headed out the door.

While I was on my way to the field, Sal saw me and yelled for me to give him a hand. He needed someone with a strong back to help unload the delivery truck. I looked at my watch. I was sure everyone was at the field waiting for me, but I couldn't leave Sal alone to do it. We had all the supplies unloaded in about an hour and I rushed over to the field. As I approached the field I thought to myself that maybe everybody went home, but then I saw my buddy Tony's jersey. I figured he either walked off without it or they were around somewhere because Tony never played football without his favorite jersey. I yelled out but no one answered. I looked around and decided to head out onto the field.

When I got closer to the middle of the field where the grass was slightly higher, I saw something. I kept walking and could make out what appeared to be a body. Then I saw the blood. Oh God, it was Tony lying in the grass. At first I thought this was one of my buddy's sick jokes and they were getting me back for being so late.

I said,

"Haha, real funny!"

Tony wasn't responding and he wasn't breathing. I called his name again because now this was just creepy. We were always playing tricks on each other but this looked too weird, even for us. I stood over him telling him, "I'm sorry I was late! Cut it out!" He didn't move. I kneeled down by him and there it was. I saw what appeared to be multiple gunshot wounds. I grabbed him in my arms still half wondering if my friend could be this cruel. Nothing like this ever happens in this safe little town.

I stood up and as I looked around, I saw Sam. He lay there on his stomach with his head turned in my direction. A look of terror was on his face and he was covered in blood. I could feel the tears and the pain in my gut. This was not a stunt. My friends had been slaughtered here in this field, the field where we played football every weekend. I stumbled around, screaming for help. Who was I kidding? We were on the outskirts of a little town and nobody would hear my shrieks. Who could have done this? Then even more unimaginable terror hit me, Brian! I yelled his name over and over again as I ran through the field but saw no sign of him, the worst thoughts going through my head. Somehow I pulled it together long enough to realize that I needed to get help but I had to find my little brother.

I ran back into town, not even noticing that I was covered in my friends' blood. I reached my house, burst through the door screaming Brian's name and grabbing the phone. I scared my mom so bad that I heard her drop a dish. I ran through the house like a madman. Mom grabbed me, screaming:

"What's going on? There's blood all over you!"

I yelled,

"I have to find Brian! Where's Brian?"

I tried to dial 911 but was too shaky.

Mom grabbed the phone from me.

I said,

"Call for help. They need an ambulance and police!"

"Who Peter? Where?" she demanded.

In my panic I didn't hear her say anything. Having heard the commotion, Brian came rushing down with his headphones hanging around his neck.

"WHAT!" he yelled.

Apparently, Mom had enough of Brian not finishing his chores and as punishment she told him he couldn't go play football. His laziness saved his life.

I cannot explain to you the relief I felt but I had to get back to the field. I grabbed him sobbing, not realizing how I must have looked to him. I was crying uncontrollably. I told Mom that I had gone to the field to meet the guys and found Tony and Sam murdered. I told her to take me back to the field. She got her car keys and we ran out the door. Mom didn't know what to say to me as I rocked back and forth in the passenger side of her car. She wanted to know what happened.

"I don't know!" I screamed.

She backed off.

As we approached the field, there were lights all over the place. Of course we couldn't get close so I jumped out of the car and began to run towards the scene. I was stopped by an officer who told me I couldn't go any closer. In my frantic state of mind I got out of hand. Two officers were now restraining me. It seemed that Tank had shown up at the field late also and called the police immediately. Of course they noticed my blood soaked clothes and hands. They demanded to know what I had done. One of the local farmers, who owned land nearby, spotted me and began pointing and yelling at the officers,

"That's him! That's the kid I saw running from the field!"

The Sheriff took one look at me and hearing that I had been at the field, immediately placed me under arrest. I was cuffed and read my rights on the way to the patrol vehicle.

I tried to explain to him that I had found them.

"Why didn't you call the authorities instead of fleeing the scene?" he asked.

"I didn't have a cell phone on me because we were meeting to play football and I didn't want to lose it," I told him.

As we entered the station I was escorted to a room and left there handcuffed. I overheard them talking, saying they were sending officers to my parents' house to search for the weapon.

"Do they really believe I did this?" I wondered.

I was angry that they wouldn't tell me anything. About twenty minutes later, two officers came into the interrogation room. I felt like my heart had stopped beating. I couldn't speak.

They began to ask me questions and I told them everything from the beginning to the end. I told them about going to the bank and helping my boss unload a truck and then I went to the field. I answered all of their questions but I could tell they didn't believe me. I was covered in the blood of my friends who had just been killed for no reason. I was exhausted, scared, and grieving and then I thought about Brian walking down the staircase and I felt some relief but that soon passed away.

My story made no sense to them. They tried to make me confess to this crime. They demanded I tell them where the murder weapon was. I told them,

"I did not do this! I don't know where the murder weapon is!"

After hours of being interrogated I was informed I was being charged with two counts of murder. I became numb. This was not happening. I was fingerprinted and booked, my clothes collected and tests run on my hands to check for gunshot residue. Then I was led away. I could hear my mom and now my dad yelling. I was being locked away with my grief and an overwhelming fear. What was going to happen to me and what the heck had happened out there on that field? What had happened to my friends? Why was I being blamed for murdering people who were like brothers to me? I also wondered if my family believed me.

I was placed in the county jail and left there, not allowed to see anyone. I heard news of the funerals of my friends. I was brokenhearted that not only was I being blamed for their murders but that I couldn't go to be with them one last time. I read a news article, "Town Torn Apart with Grief as They Mourn for Two of Their Own." There was a picture of Tank in the caption, supported by his parents as he doubled over with sorrow. There was also a mugshot of me, at which I turned away. How could any of this be happening to us?

My dad hired a lawyer friend of his, Raphael Maren, to represent me. He was a sharp middle-aged man with ordinary looks and a chiseled jaw. I walked him through everything, answered all of his questions, and he responded with compassion. I knew that from telling him about my trip to the bank and then helping my boss out that I would be out of there in no time. I had an alibi.

"The prosecutor is saying that even with that, you had more than enough time to commit the crimes. They're saying you did those things to try to throw the police off."

He then looked me in the eye and said,

"Peter, they're seeking the death penalty for you."

I thought up to that point that life could not get any worse but hearing those words proved me wrong. I grabbed my head. I guess I thought if I squeezed hard enough, I could wake from this nightmare but there was no relief for me.

In that instant I flashed back to just a few years back when I sat in the woods with a gun to my head. I wished I had just killed myself then. I remembered that voice that said,

"Peace, be still."

If I could have found the strength in me now, I would have laughed at that. What peace could I have? What peace would my family have? God, how I despised myself for not having been man enough to pull the trigger!

Anger, Despair, Depression: Oh My!

When I was arrested, I think I was the angriest I had ever been up to that point in my young life. I kept thinking, why don't people believe me when I'm telling the truth? Every time I was confronted with the murders of my friends it made me rage inside like a bull. Not only was I the accused and being held without bail, but was denied any opportunity to grieve for them. I couldn't go to their funerals. I was taken away from my family. I was the devil to a community who loved these young men. I knew that I was innocent. I had lost my friends because someone out there hated them enough to kill them. I knew it wasn't me!

No one seemed to care about what was happening to me. How do I live with the nightmare of seeing my friends murdered like that? I had no one to talk to about it because my lawyer told me not to say a word. I understood that, but still had no means of handling what had happened. I could never say goodbye. Every time I closed my eyes I saw blood, their blood. I tried to counter these thoughts with the fact that my brother and Tank were still alive. I was so thankful for their lives being spared.

I had knots in my stomach wondering what my family really thought. I was unable to see or talk to anyone but my lawyer for about a month and I thought that alone would kill me. I needed for my family to believe that they did not raise a killer. I missed my little brother most of all. I thought about the times we would hang out and go swimming at the creek or the times when we would blare our music so loud Mom or Dad would come banging on our door with shoes for us to turn it down. I thought back to how my mom and brother (and at times my dad) would sing me "happy birthday." No matter how many birthdays came, Brian would always reach his hand into the cake, dig out a huge chunk and throw it at me. I think this was his version of baptism. When he first began doing that, both of us would be yelled at but as years went on, it was just a known thing that he would do this and only on my birthday. I loved my brother. It worried me that I might not see him go out on his first date or see him go to his prom.

I was placed on suicide watch after receiving a letter from my friend Jimmy. I thought to myself,

"If I didn't have the guts to do it that night in the woods, why now?"

When I got that letter and saw the name on it, I can't even tell you how I saw that as a ray of light. I was receiving so much hate mail and so many death threats that I eventually stopped looking at my mail, but this was a treat. Jimmy and I hung out a lot and even though I thought of Tony being my best friend, Jimmy was right up there. I think we weren't as close as Tony and I because Jimmy had gone away to college right after high school graduation. He was the smartest person I knew besides my dad. He excelled at everything he did. Tank was the "go-to guy" when you needed a date but Jimmy was the one you went to for help in school.

I opened his letter with such happiness. I was thrilled that someone familiar had reached out to me. I was shocked to see that Jimmy had nothing kind to say. I have since thrown his letter away but the words were etched on my heart. He wrote:

Peter,

You no good murderer! How could you do something like this to guys who loved you? I hate you so much for this! I seriously hope they fry you for this and I can sit and watch. I hope you rot in hell for what you have done!

Reading those words from someone that I loved was it! I lay down on my bed, closed my eyes and slept for days. I think I thought if I just lay there long enough I would just die in my sleep. This nightmare of being blamed for something that I was grieving over myself was too much for me to deal with. I needed someone to help me, or I needed to just die and be done with it all.

The Iron Cage

If you have never been to prison, you are blessed. It is a world that is full of darkness and the deepest despair you could ever imagine. Since the town I lived in couldn't house a big-time accused "murderer" like me I was shipped two hundred miles away from my family to one of the most violent prisons imaginable. As a twenty year old man, you think about what you wish you could be doing and places you wish you were. My life was now a cage.

The first thing they do to you in prison is strip search you. They make you take everything off and they inspect every cavity of your body, including making you squat and cough, looking for any drugs, contraband or weapons. This is the beginning of your humanity being taken from you. You are then assigned a number. No more will you be known by your name. You are tagged like an animal. You are now a number belonging to the state. The reason for being reduced to a number, in my opinion, is to strip you of your identity. After all, isn't that what happened to Daniel, Hananiah, Mishael, and Azariah in the book of Daniel? When they were taken captive, they were stripped of their birth names and given new names, heathen names, to show them that they were being placed under subjection in a new system. Our names are who we are. Thank God those Hebrew boys knew who they were!

The floor of a prison cell is cold as it is, of course, not carpeted. The bed that you lie on is a smelly, nasty thing not meant to make you feel like you are in a spa retreat.

Prison is cold, dirty and it is never, ever quiet. In my stay, I have seen young guys like me go absolutely insane and have to be medicated because of the constant noise. The worst thing is never knowing when violence will break out. On any given day there are fights, stabbings and I have even heard of murders taking place. While I was there two people committed suicide.

The gangs are plentiful and if you do not choose which side you want to be on, you are pretty much a target. It was always fascinating to me to see the control the gangs had. You would think the prison administration would dismantle all of that but the people in charge pretty much look the other way as long as they don't start fights. If a large enough fight does start, that's when you see the riot gear show up and that disarming march that they do. It sounds like soldiers marching for battle. It is done to intimidate, which it does. When the officers have to go in to break things up and have to go so far as bringing out the riot squad, as soon as I would hear that uniform march, it struck fear in me.

Being a young kid who knew I didn't belong there I chose to not pick any gang to affiliate with, which sometimes left me vulnerable. Somehow I was pretty much able to talk my way out of things and stay out of fights. All I wanted to do was go home, but home seemed like a faraway dream, and I was smack dab in the middle of my own personal nightmare.

Let me describe the mundane nature of prison. Each day you do the same thing over and over again. Think of being forced to fold a towel again and again, over and over.

It's the same towel and you have to fold it the same way each time. There's no color to it to make you even appreciate looking at it. That is what prison is. You wear the same clothes as everybody else. You wear the same shoes as everybody else. You are told to eat when everybody else eats, sleep when everybody else sleeps, then get up the next morning and do it all over again. I can't even imagine what lifers go through in their mind each day.

I tried to busy myself with going to programs when volunteers came in to hold classes. They were my only contact with the outside world and I appreciated being able to look at the different clothes they wore because at least I could see something new. I know that sounds weird but when all of your freedoms are stripped from you and you find yourself looking at the same drab colors, you find different ways to remind yourself that you are still alive and a human being.

In prison it is not just the inmates you have to watch, but there are some officers that let the power go to their head and you have to be careful in their presence. Some of them are fair in how they deal with the inmates and there were even those that I could see had a relationship with Christ. They were firm and no nonsense, but they were kind. It's easy to focus on the bad ones when you are in a place like this. Once I became a Christian, I learned to pray for everyone, not just those who treated me kindly.

There was one particular bully who misused his authority on a regular basis, and I did not escape his wrath. This man seemed to hate all of humanity! He did everything in his power to intimidate me, but I think because I was young and I was also bitter from this experience I gave it right back. That was not the wise thing to do. He had the power and he knew it. I received two misconducts which resulted in a trip to the hole and they tacked on more time. I finally realized that I was only hurting myself. I had been locked up for a horrendous crime that I had nothing to do with and now I was becoming my own worst enemy. When he began to see that I would not fight back anymore he moved on to his next victim. I will always "fondly" remember him as "Terror Behind a Badge." I thought it was fitting because his last name was Terrie.

Now this next thing I talk about may make some uncomfortable and maybe that's a good thing. I have witnessed guys being raped by other guys and I almost became a statistic myself. Homosexual activity in prison is off the charts and should be a sound reason for a heterosexual man to do everything he can to stay out. For all you "wannabe" thugs that think you are the man, there is someone locked up waiting for you. I'm trying to warn you to change your life. You may be tough on the streets but I have seen gang leaders succumb to the sexual depravity of prison. There is no worse fear than to have something that you should be able to control, such as your own body, used for things that are too horrible to even pen in this book.

Men who have families back home and wives that they love turn themselves over to their own lusts and do things that they never imagined they would do. I talked to one such man. He seemed to be a nice guy and before he was arrested he was very successful. He and his business partner built a computer company from scrap and, over time, turned it into a thriving business. Their company was always being mentioned in one business magazine or another. His problem was that he became greedy. As the company expanded he told me that he wanted more and more. He married a beautiful, successful doctor and they had two children. He said that the lifestyle he had become accustomed to was fast boats, several luxury homes and the best of everything. The only problem was that he was spending more than his company was bringing in. He said he was so in love with his wife that he would do anything for her and what he loved most was to lavish her with stuff, expensive stuff.

He said that she wanted to stay home with the children and he supported that because he was doing so well, but the trap was that he never had enough. He thought he could go it alone, that this would mean more money for him. One person stood in the way of his dream, however: his partner. He told me that he hatched a plan to make his partner of ten years vanish. He began setting a paperwork trail to make it look like his partner was stealing money. They were working late one night and went into the basement to go over some inventory. Apparently this basement had a small, unused classroom and that's where he shot his partner in cold blood. He then took the body out to his truck, drove to the water's edge and dumped him in. During the investigation his story didn't add up and after a long trial, here he sits, a married man who is now another man's boyfriend.

I actually was bold enough to ask him if he felt like he was cheating on his wife or if he was homosexual or bisexual. I was just trying to understand this. He said that he had never had any interest in another man and he felt that because he was not with another woman, he wasn't cheating. He ended this conversation by saying that being a married man, he was used to being close to his wife and being intimate with her. He said,

"She's not here but this man is."

He told me that he will never get out of prison and even though he still loves his wife this is his life now and he accepts that.

This conversation had me spinning. He was an intelligent man who had it all, but in his opinion, he had to alter his mind to accept things as they have been given to him. He said that he was guilty and rather than fantasize about freedom, he would take what he could get in prison. In our chats, he would speak of his wife often and let it be known that she comes to see him. It's crazy to me that he can sit with her and say he loves her while wearing such a dishonest mask.

The yard was a world that I could never have imagined either. I would stand against the wall of the prison and watch in absolute awe at the strangeness of what I was seeing. In the yard, you have all of these different groups. There are the Latinos who are divided by gang affiliation, the African Americans who are divided by gang affiliation and the skinheads and pedophiles who are hated by all. Then there is everyone else of every ethnic and financial background. Hatred and division seem to be the common ground in prison. I always looked at this with amazement because one group always felt superior to the other group, even though we were all wearing the same uniform. We were all locked up and we were all at the mercy of people with power over us.

Being out in the yard was dangerous, because there was always the threat of violence. I figured it out long ago that the safest place for me was against the wall. It was a bloody place to be but I enjoyed being out in the fresh air.

Whether there was violence or not I loved being in the sun and not having my nostrils accosted by the stench of the prison.

I had many different cellies but there was a short period of time that I went without one. This was like gold to me. To have the small, inferior space to myself was like a little piece of heaven. The different personalities that are housed together pose a difficulty, because you may get someone that you get along with great but once they go off to another prison, you wonder, what next? I think I've had my share of people I didn't get along with more than those that I did. The best guy I ever shared a space with was named Gabe. He was a very interesting fellow (to say the least.)

Gabe

I was in transition to have another cellmate and going through the usual stress of wondering who I would get. Well, one day I was in the cafeteria and had just picked up my tray. I turned around and about fifteen feet from me, I saw it. An unwelcome visitor from my past dreams had now invaded my "awake" time. As I turned, I spotted the black robe with the "S" embroidered on the chest, dripping with blood. At first I thought this was some dumb joke being played on me, but a split second later I realized that I had never shared my dreams with anyone here. I could not see a face as the hood draped it. The terrifying figure glided toward me with speed. I heard a voice that I have not heard since I was a child. It sent chills up and down my spine. I heard it say,

"You belong to me!"

And it literally passed through me.

The next thing I knew I dropped my tray and screamed in agony, gripped by overwhelming fear. Who else would be working the cafeteria but "Officer Terror," I mean Terrie! He laughed and accused me of causing a commotion and, with three other officers, I was escorted to the hole. Day and night the voice played in my head and I felt like I was becoming a madman. The prison staff tried to medicate me but there are always ways of getting around actually taking the medication. I spent five long days of hell in the hole. Finally they took me back to my cell.

When I arrived there, Terror pushed me in and I almost fell to the floor. I looked over at the small desk and there was my new cellie. Once I caught myself before hitting the ground, I stood up straight and looked at the new guy. Some of my cellmates I wondered if they were guilty or if they were like me, wrongly accused. Others I didn't have to wonder too much about. This guy was different from all of them. He was tall, clean cut and rather muscular. He looked scholarly and was quite articulate. I didn't have the nerve to ask him what he was there for. He smiled, extended his hand, and told me his name was Gabe.

We got the introductions out of the way and didn't say a whole lot to each other for the rest of the afternoon. Gabe was busy writing. He spent what seemed to be all day and all night writing letters. I just assumed he was working on his case and maybe writing family. Whenever I walked into the cell, there was Gabe, like a machine, writing with his worn Bible by his side.

The next day I talked to him about my "incident" in the cafeteria. I don't know why I felt the need to talk to him. His eyes made me feel that it was safe to tell him anything. He would stop writing and give me his full attention. Talking to him made time fly by and I realized that he was very different from everyone else there. I will admit one thing: this was the first time I had a cellie that even owned a Bible and I was just waiting for him to begin hitting me upside my head with Bible verses. Strangely enough, he didn't. He would listen to me and then when I was done, he talked to me like he'd known me all my life. From time to time, he would share a Scripture and show me where it was in the Bible. But this guy was like an open Bible. He had it in him and I could tell from the way he talked that he lived it. But what was he doing locked up with the rest of us so- called "animals?"

I started off by saying these words which I never uttered again to him:

"You're probably gonna think I'm crazy for saying this."

Gabe stopped me right there and said,

"Peter, don't ever think that anything you say would make me think you are crazy. I have seen a lot in my travels so there isn't much that shocks me."

He laughed slightly, so I told him about what I saw in the cafeteria. He asked me how I was feeling now and I guess because I'm a man and men are not supposed to show fear, I said,

"I'm fine."

Gabe looked at me and it was as though I could see fire in his eyes. He said,

"Let's get one thing straight here. If you don't want to be honest, you cannot be helped."

He then put his head back down to what he had been writing. I was stunned! My first thought was, who does this dude think he is? My second was: he's right.

I sat on my bunk and about three minutes later, I said to him,

"I'm scared."

He stopped writing and said,

"Now we can proceed."

When he said that, I wondered if this guy had been a therapist or something, which made me smile. I imagined myself stretched out on a couch, pouring out my heart to him while he took notes. He listened to what I had to say and with his next words he had my complete attention. He asked me if I remembered when I was a boy and my mom taking me to church. I said I remembered a little bit of that. He then asked me if I remembered how fascinated I was with the Cross that hung behind the preacher. My mouth dropped! I hadn't thought about that in many years. How could Gabe know anything about this?

My thoughts turned instantly to my parents. I thought my dad had been able to smuggle in my own private shrink or something. There was just no way he could have known about this. He didn't give me a chance to answer because he saw the look on my face. He went on to say to me "You were always drawn to the Cross because you knew that there was something special about it." He said that he understood I didn't learn much of its worth at church but that my grandparents had made us go and shared as much with me as they could about Jesus in the short time I would visit. I continued to sit there, shocked and riveted! WHO THE HECK WAS HE?

Gabe grabbed for his Bible and turned to Romans 10: 9. He handed it to me for me to read. I read it quietly to myself and then tried to hand it back to him. He said,

"Read it out loud. It may help you understand what it is saying"

So I did.

> *"That if thou shalt confess with thy mouth the Lord Jesus, and shalt believe in thine heart that*

God hath raised Him from the dead, thou shalt be saved."

I handed it back to him. Gabe looked at me with boundless compassion and said,

"Peter, the reason you were drawn to that Cross is because a day was coming when Christ would reveal Himself to you. That day is today."

He continued,

"The Cross that you were so drawn to represented the Cross that Jesus was nailed to. He was nailed to it and hung there to pay for the sins of humanity. The Scripture you just read means that because He died and rose for you, you and anyone else can freely come to Him and be forgiven of your sins. In other words, He exchanged His perfect life for your tattered, sinful life. All you have to do is invite Him into your heart and believe that God raised Him from the dead. He gave His life because He loves you."

He sat back in his chair and didn't say another word seeing the tears in my eyes. I laid down on my cot and as the tears fell to my pillow, I drifted off to sleep. The words I had just read echoed in my heart and wrapped themselves around me.

At some point, I was awakened by the same terrifying voice I've heard before. It was a horrible, bewitching voice that said,

"You'll never escape. You belong to me!"

I heard it as though someone was next to me, speaking directly into my ear. I woke up in a cold sweat, panting as though I had just run a marathon. I looked around frantically to try and figure out where I was and there was Gabe looking over at me from the desk.

"Dreams getting to you again?" he asked.

I said,

"Something like that."

Then I asked him if I could talk to him about my dreams. He gave me his undivided attention.

I told him how I had been tormented since I was a child and said that the dreams always seemed so real to the point that at times, I woke up with scratches on my arms or marks around my neck.

"Why did it seem so real when it was just a dream? Was I actually the one doing those things to myself?" I asked.

"They seem real because they are real. The marks on your body were physical manifestations of what was being done TO you not BY you," he replied.

Then he did it again. He blew my mind. He asked me if I had ever heard about the supernatural realm. I looked at him, puzzled. Gabe explained that the supernatural realm is as real as what we see in this earth.

"Peter, if God were to open your eyes right now and allow you to see what is all around you, you would see many things not of this earth."

Well, that kind of freaked me out but because I have had these unwelcome nightmares all of my life, I listened.

He continued,

"A person is made up of three parts, body, soul and spirit. Even when you are asleep, the spirit is still alert and very sensitive to what is going on. It can interact with the spirit realm. Your torment began at an early age because you were a child. Children are very sensitive to the supernatural even though they do not understand what is going on. It is a child's innocence that enables them to easily feel and see what many adults cannot. That is why parents should listen to their children when they tell them about monsters in their room. A child describes a demon as a monster because that is what they are familiar with. Monsters are frightening to children, but what they are really seeing is a demonic spirit so they associate the two."

"Whoa, now Gabe!" I said.

"What do you mean demons? You mean witches riding around on broomsticks or goblin type images, because that's not what I was seeing!"

Gabe chuckled.

"No, Peter. Demons are exactly what you were being tormented by throughout your life. Think back and remember what they looked like and what they smelled like. Remember the darkness that was not of this world and the way they sounded."

As he spoke, I began to go back to that ugly place and I didn't like it. One thing I had to ask him was this,

"If God is so loving, why does He allow innocent children to be tormented like that?"

Gabe sat back in his chair.

"Peter, nothing, and I mean nothing, can happen without God's permission and because of that, God is always in control. All things happen for a reason. Do you think you were the only child who had that experience?"

I honestly didn't know how to answer that. He said,

"Remember what you're dealing with, because one day you will help other people, especially children, through their own torment."

He looked at me and said,

"Peter, don't ever underestimate who you are because you will do much work for the Lord."

I said to him,

"I don't believe in God. I grew up in a home where God was never relevant."

I told him about my dad's belongings that were passed down to him from his father and the pentagram necklace that Dad always had around his neck. Gabe looked me in the eye and said,

"Peter, you are the one who will change your generation."

Those words were a bit much for me. Here I am sitting in prison for the murder of my friends and he's talking to me like I'm some kind of superhero. I said,

"Yeah, okay, whatever!"

At that point, I thought I was done with this conversation and then Gabe said something else that grabbed at me.

"Why didn't you pull the trigger?" he questioned.

I thought he was talking about the crime.

"I could have never hurt my friends. That's why!" I snapped.

"No Peter. When you sat alone against the tree with the gun to your head, what happened? Why didn't you pull the trigger that night?" he asked.

My mouth was hanging open. How did he know this? I hadn't shared that with anyone in this miserable place because the last thing you want anyone in prison to think is that you are weak.

"Who are you?" I asked.

"My name is Gabriel and it really isn't important who I am. What is important is that you learn who you are."

He told me,

"Your life was spared that night and it wasn't because you chickened out. You received a divine intervention from Someone who loves you so much that He gave His life for you."

I could feel myself trembling but it was a good tremble.

"Who are you talking about Gabe?"

He said,

"I'm talking about Jesus. When you were small and sitting in church staring at the Cross, you pondered it in your heart and had many questions about it. The night you heard His voice, Jesus' voice, you were introduced to the One who hung on that Cross."

I knew that the words he was speaking were true. The only thing I liked about being in church was the Cross and the few times it had ever been discussed. I began to pace our tiny cell and rub my head at the same time. I asked Gabe,

"How can this be happening to me when I am facing the death penalty? Does Jesus want to save me because He knows I'm going to die in this place?"

Gabe watched, seemingly amused. Then he responded,

"Peter, you will not die in this place. You will be broken and reborn in this place."

He went back to the desk and began writing. I didn't know what was happening. My mind was racing like lightning. I finally broke the silence and asked,

"Gabe, why would Jesus want me? I'm so screwed up. I didn't exactly grow up in a household where God was talked about. My parents for most of my life thought I was crazy. I wasn't very loving to my parents when I got older. I did drugs. I drank. I had sex with lots of girls. From what little I've heard about Jesus, He doesn't exactly like that stuff. Why would He love me? Was prison my punishment for everything that I did that Jesus didn't like?"

Gabe got up from his desk and sat by me on my cot. He answered,

"Peter, you are just the kind of person that God is looking for. He knows your heart and nothing that you have ever done has ever surprised Him. He knows your beginning from your end and He does love you."

I said to him,

"Well, maybe I need to start cleaning myself up first and then I can talk to God."

He replied,

"It doesn't work that way Peter. First, go to God and then let Him do the cleaning up."

I shook my head in protest saying,

"I'm not good enough to hang out with God."

Gabe responded,

"No one is good enough to hang out with Him, but His presence inside of a person allows them to hang out with Him. The first step is to ask Him into your heart."

I said,

"Gabe, I'm not ready. This is too much."

He looked at me and said,

"I know you're not ready, YET."

They called for lights out. Gabe got up and hopped onto his cot and I laid down, deep in thought. He said one more thing to me before the quiet fell.

"Peter, always remember this: With God the story of your life is already finished, and nothing catches Him off guard. Picture your life as a beautiful painting created by Him. God isn't in heaven holding a big eraser every time you mess up.

Your mess ups and all of your accomplishments are already painted and it is all one beautiful picture."

All throughout my sleep, I was dreaming about the night I put that gun to my head. It was like I was standing there watching myself. I saw the anguish in my own eyes and I felt the helplessness of my own heart. I walked closer and looked into my eyes. They looked dead. All of a sudden, as I stood there watching, remembering what I was thinking that night and at that moment, I saw this bright flash of light. In this light, I heard the most beautiful voice I had ever heard before, "Peace, be still." And then the light was gone. As I stood there watching myself put the gun down, I was amazed. I don't remember seeing a light when this actually occurred. I looked around but didn't see anyone. The peace I was feeling at that moment was like the sound of that voice. In the dream, I smiled and then I woke up.

When I looked around, I could see that it was daytime. Although it was morning, the prison was strangely quiet. This never happens. There is always noise and screaming and things banging around. This time, it was peaceful. I got up and just assumed that Gabe was still sleeping and I looked over at the desk. I walked over and saw tons of letters but I did not want to violate his trust by reading them. I felt great respect for this man, whoever he was. I moved some of them and uncovered the Bible. I just wondered, if I had an encounter with God that night in the woods, were those words somewhere in this Bible?

For someone who is untrained in Scriptures just picking up a Bible can be an intimidating feeling. When I saw how heavy and thick it was, I wondered how I could possibly navigate through it. I said to myself "there is no way I'm going to find those three little words in such a huge book." As I fingered through it, I noticed it had an index in the back so I thought it might help to look up the word "peace." After scrolling down, I saw what might be the precise Scripture. It said Mark 4:39. Unsure how to find Mark, I flipped to the front and found every book of the Bible with a page number. Got it! I went to the page and I read. When I got to the words, the room brightened. It was like I was outside in the sunshine. I read those words and then pulled the Bible to my heart. And then I heard my last name called.

"James! James! Wake up. Your attorney's here to see you."

I had been asleep the whole time. It was all a dream. It was a great dream. I shook myself to wake up some more and then got ready to talk to my attorney. I knew from all these good things happening to me that my lawyer was coming to tell me they had found the person or people responsible for killing my friends and I was going home!

Dis-Appointments

I went into the small room where my attorney sat. He didn't have anything new or anything good to tell me. It looked like I would be going to trial for two counts of murder and my punishment would be death, if found guilty. How could this be happening after such a good dream?

My attorney told me that we needed to begin preparing for court and we went over all of the evidence the state said they had against me. According to the state, I had plenty of time to commit the murders. I was also found covered in my friends' blood, and there was a witness who saw me flee the scene. My attorney said that they had no motive. I said,

"Of course not, because I didn't kill my friends!"

I looked at him and implored him to look me in the eyes and tell me that he believed me. I needed to know that the person who had my future in his hands was at least on my side.

"I'm working for you and I am going to fight with everything in me to prove your innocence," he said.

He then sat back and said that my family was not handling this well.

"Your dad has told me about your childhood and the times that you were violent. He talked about taking you to psychiatrists and how you would always tell them about seeing monsters."

I looked at him and said,

"Please don't tell me you are going to try to say that I am insane. I'm not."

He could tell that I did not want to talk to him about this but he told me that he needed to know everything. I told him everything that my parents told him and he looked worried. I said,

"Attorney Maren, I am not crazy! I know it sounds really bad but these things were really happening to me."

He said,

"I'm concerned the state might obtain this information and use it against you and argue, that in a crazed fit of rage, you killed those two young men."

I wondered if life could get any worse than this. I must admit I was very angry with my parents. Even in my upset state I wanted to know how they were. I hadn't seen them since I came to prison and wanted to know if they had gotten my letters. I could tell that he didn't want to get into this but he answered my questions.

"They got the letters. Your family is preparing to move because people in the town have become so confrontational with them. Your brother had to be taken out of school, your mom was afraid to leave the house, and your father has taken early retirement because of the non- stop harassment he faced daily."

This tore me apart! I guess I never really stopped to think about how this was affecting my family, because I was so worried about myself.

"Please tell my family to come see me."

He promised that he would and then we got back to business. I felt more determined than ever to prove my innocence and protect my family. Our meeting ended and I went back to my cell. I was worn out and just wanted to lie down, but Gabe was in the mood to chat.

"Hey Peter, how'd your meeting go?" he asked.

"My parents told my attorney about my terror dreams, and my attorney thinks I'm crazy."

Gabe looked at me and said,

"How come you haven't told me all of your dreams?"

I looked at him confused and said,

"What are you talking about Gabe?"

He said,

"I thought you would be anxious to talk to me about the old lady."

Again, I was shocked.

"Since you brought her up, you tell me."

Gabe smiled and asked,

"Do you know who she was?"

I said,

"I don't but was always curious about that."

He said,

"Before I tell you who she is, let's first talk about something else. You have another recurring dream that you haven't mentioned. Let's talk about the group wearing the black robes."

Although I had been drained after meeting with my attorney, I felt a new gust of strength. I told him everything that I could remember about that dream, sat back, and waited for him to respond.

"All of your dreams are connected. The group doing the sacrifice, were very heavily into the occult. Your father's mother and father were Satan worshippers. Your grandfather was the leader of this group! The "S" on the robe stood for Satan."

He looked at me with a seriousness in his eyes and said,

"Peter, before you were born, a demonic prophesy was spoken over you that you would be the human sacrifice to carry on the blood of Satan. When it came down to it, your dad couldn't kill you so he fled along with your mom."

I was beyond stunned. I threw my hands up and said,

"WAIT! What do you mean I was supposed to be a sacrifice? They wanted to kill me?"

He answered with:

"Part of the reason your dad moved the family around so much was because he had a fear of his father. His dad had become so angry at him for not shedding your blood for Satan that your father disconnected from all of his family and that's why you never really got to know them. Didn't you find it strange that your parents never allowed your grandparents to be around you alone, and that your visits were brief and very few?"

"I never thought about that. All I knew was that my grandparents were drunks and very violent people," I said.

Gabe replied,

"Peter, your grandparents drank the way they did because that was how they coped with the evil they invited into their lives. They pretty much killed themselves because that is what Satan does. When your father refused to give you over to him, the demonic activity in your grandparents' lives became more violent because Satan was demanding a sacrifice."

I asked,

"Was that why my grandfather died and my grandmother ended up in a mental institution?"

Gabe said,

"Sadly, yes."

He continued,

"Your father's parents served Satan with a fierceness and they were very loyal to him. Satan will promise you the world as long as he can control you but your father, in a way, double crossed him by saving your life. Don't think for a moment that your dad did not know that the torment you were going through was real. He just didn't know how to help you. Your dad tried to walk away from the occult, but by not turning to Jesus, he was left without any instruction on how to fight the supernatural. Your dad felt that if he didn't believe in anything, it would be better than believing in the devil. This is the other reason why you moved around so much. Your dad didn't know how to help you but thought he could outrun Satan to keep you safe."

I sat there trying to process all of this. I said,

"So all those times my dad seemed so disconnected from me, he just didn't know how to help me?"

Gabe said,

"That is true but Peter, understand that your father grew up in a loveless home himself. It's hard to give love when you have never received love."

When Gabe said those words to me, I felt a lot of the anger that I had towards my father melt away. I asked him,

"What can you tell me about the old lady? Why is she significant?"

Gabe smiled at me again and said,

"That old lady is your great, great, great grandmother, on your mother's side. Her name is Hannah. She was a woman of great faith and loved God with all her heart. She was also visited by dreams in which God would show her things to come. Because of her prayers and her faith, she would change things in her family."

He paused and looked at me.

I asked him if she was praying for anything in particular. Gabe stated, "She was praying for you! God would show her the evil that would mingle its darkness into her family line and she would pray for God to raise up a curse breaker. When you saw her praying, she was praying for you that you would come to know Christ and do the work that He has called for your hands to do."

He went on saying,

"All of those tormenting things that you experienced and the lack of love in your family, the satanic rituals, the rage, the drug and alcohol abuse and more are curses in your family line. God does not want His people to be destroyed by them. In every generation, there is someone that God places His hand on to be the one, through the power of the Holy Spirit, to stop those curses from continuing in their family line. Not only that but once the curse is stopped, the blessings of God can be released in the family. Peter, you were born to break the curse."

How could I deny any of this? This man just sat here, once again, and told me things that I never shared with anyone. At that point, there was a call for "Lights Out." I laid down and pondered everything that I had been told. I drifted off into a peaceful sleep and there she was, my great, great, great grandmother. On her knees praying but this time, I could hear her. She prayed with such heartfelt emotions, crying out to God. I heard her thank Him for His faithfulness and for allowing her to be His daughter. She said,

"Lord, You have shown me the evil coming to my family but Lord, You have also promised that You would raise up someone to destroy the evil works of Satan. Lord I pray for him. Raise him up. Guide him and strengthen him. Lord God when his test comes before him, don't let him faint. Show him that greater is He that is in him than he that is in the world. Show him while he is in the midst of his test, who he is."

Then I saw the pages of the old photograph book begin to blow, as the gentle wind blew through her room as it always did. What was different this time, however, was that when it got to the photograph that I could never make out, there I was. Everything in this photo was clear to me. I was standing at the top of what looked like a mountain. I looked to be about the age I am now. I stood there and just stared at my picture. I then heard her say,

"Run to Jesus!"

I turned back to her but she didn't seem to know I was there. She said,

"He is there with His arms open. Run to Jesus."

When I came out of the dream, I remember hearing myself saying,

"Jesus. Here I am. Here I am."

I realized I was weeping and my hands were lifted.

I Surrender

I'd only been with Gabe for seven days but it felt like he had taught me a lifetime worth of wisdom. I became very close to him and I can't even tell you the respect I developed for him. Whenever I looked at Gabe, I saw someone who was incredibly strong in his belief. I just couldn't believe that someone like him would be in prison. We never discussed why he was there, or whether he was innocent. I did finally ask him what was with all the writing. The guy never took a break. All he said was that they were messages that he would someday deliver to the people whom they were written for. I thought he meant that he was some kind of a preacher because he sure did know a lot about me and he really touched my heart.

"Peter, there is a man who comes here every Monday. His name is Pastor Jonathan. He does a service here in the prison. This is a service that you really need to get plugged into and God will use Pastor Jonathan to teach you many things. He is a very faithful servant of God and also very gracious. He will be here tonight at 7:45, to do a men's service."

I asked if he would go with me. He said,

"I have something else I need to do, but this is a very important service for you to attend."

I said okay and went out to the yard to get some much needed exercise.

When they called for the service, I eagerly got in line and approached the classroom. Almost every seat was taken and then there were men sitting on the piano bench and on a couple tables that were out. Pastor Jonathan was standing there at the podium greeting everyone like old friends as they came in. You could clearly see the love that this man had in his heart for each one of these men and that he was excited about being here.

He wasn't at all what I expected a preacher to look like. I thought I'd walk in and see a much older white man wearing a collar and black suit. This was all I knew from when I visited my grandparents church as a boy. As it turned out, he was a dark-skinned Hispanic man who looked to be in his mid-fifties wearing a t-shirt and jeans. I didn't know what to think.

Once everyone signed in and sat down one of the inmates stood up and went to the front. Pastor Jonathan shook his hand and then this man, Michael, opened up the service by greeting the men and welcoming everyone to church. He had tattoos on his face, neck and his arms. I'm guessing each one was significant to him. He stood probably 6'3 and was all muscle. I'm sure on the street he commanded respect. Michael had been the head of a gang and was referred to as "The Lieutenant." He had a history of being in and out of prison. I was told that he was in here this time for setting a house on fire that belonged to a rival gang leader. Inside were five small children and their mother, and all were killed. He said that out of all the gang-banging, shooting and robbing that he had done, this crime is what broke his heart the most. He stuck around to make sure his target was inside and could hear children screaming. He said he still hears them sometimes in his sleep. I noticed that when people saw him in prison, who knew him from the street and called him Lieutenant, he quickly corrected them by saying, "My name is Michael." He introduced Pastor Jonathan and said,

"Give this man of God your undivided attention."

Michael then began to read a Scripture and he prayed. The atmosphere didn't feel like prison anymore. The men were standing on their feet with their hands lifted, some crying, some praising God and some were totally out of their element like me, looking like deer in headlights.

When Michael finished praying Pastor Jonathan took the lead. He said to stay in an attitude of worship and began to sing this song that I had never heard before that really moved me. He sang with the voice of an angel. The men joined in and it easily sounded like 200 voices in there. I had never experienced anything like this before. It was certainly different from the church that I remembered as a boy. I felt so good.

When we were done singing he stood there as if waiting for something. He just lifted his hands and said,

"Come Holy Spirit. Come."

Many men were saying,

"Yes Lord. Please come and have Your way."

This went on for about three minutes and then there was quiet. Pastor Jonathan said that we could have our seats and he opened his Bible up. He looked up at the crowd and told us that God loved us and I could see some of the men smiling.

He said that God had put it in his heart to minister about salvation. He then asked the group what that meant. I thought,

"Oh boy. A question and answer period."

I was scared that he would call on me and I would look like a fool, but he just let people respond on their own. They said things like,

"It means to be saved from eternal damnation."

One guy said,

"It means we are forgiven for our sins."

Another said,

"It means Jesus lives in our hearts."

Someone else said,

"When we die, we will reign in glory with God for eternity."

Pastor Jonathan said,

"It means all of those things and more. Let's look at Romans 10:9."

I remembered Gabe mentioning that verse to me. The guy next to me saw me having trouble finding it, so he very kindly helped me. I said,

"Thanks. I'm new at this."

He smiled and welcomed me. Pastor Jonathan asked for someone to read it out loud. A man named Avery stood and read with such authority,

> *"That if thou shalt confess with thy mouth the Lord Jesus, and shalt believe in thine heart that*

> *God hath raised Him from the dead, thou shalt be saved."*

Avery then sat down. I looked over at him amazed that he was an inmate and not a preacher like Pastor Jonathan.

Then Pastor Jonathan said,

"Salvation is an action word, and I don't believe the church always does a good job explaining it."

I was actually stunned by those words. Here's a pastor saying that the church is not doing something to the fullest?

"There are churches that teach that the way to heaven is to join the church. The way to be forgiven is to come to church. The way to Jesus is to be faithful to the church. There are churches that are falsely teaching that going to heaven is directly tied to how much money we give. I grew up in a church just like that and was surprised that I still was dealing with lust and greed while serving on the various boards of the church. All that time I was having sexual relations with women in church. People knew about this and it all seemed okay."

He continued on,

"Then one day I was in a horrible car accident and was rushed to the hospital. I felt my life slipping away. I felt like I was falling and was surrounded by darkness. I began to ask Jesus why I was going to hell, and I began to tell Jesus how good a person I was. I told Him how I had done everything my pastor told me to do. I give lots of money. I'm a nice man and faithful to the church."

Jesus said,

"You are faithful to all the wrong things and you have never known Me. If you do not get to know Me, hell awaits you."

He said that he had never heard the voice of God before but knew it was Him. The Lord continued,

"You have been busy doing THINGS in the church and for that, people believe you are walking with Me, but I look at the heart. I am the way to My Father. It is not through works but through Me. Jonathan, I have loved you since before your mother and father even knew you and I am the One who paid the ultimate price for you by giving My life. The way to My father is THROUGH me. Read and study My Word and know ME."

Pastor Jonathan continued his story,

"As time passed, after a series of surgeries, I heard nurses say I was in the ICU and remember hearing a lot of noise day in and day out. Machines were keeping me alive. I kept trying to communicate with people but couldn't make a sound. I heard doctors telling my parents that there was little hope that I would recover and that they should consider removing me from life support! I was desperate to show them I was still in here and not to give up. My heart would break every time my mother began to cry. My father would have to take her out of the room. My parents were Christians, but their faith seemed to be shaken." He looked at us, with tears in his eyes and as his voice shook he said,

"The only hope I had was Jesus."

Pastor Jonathan went on to tell us that he began to tune out what the doctors were saying and he tuned out the pain coursing through his body. He was desperate to have an encounter with the Lord Jesus Christ. He told us that he wasn't sure Jesus would commune with him in his state but he had to try. He said that although no one could hear his voice he believed Jesus could and he told Him,

"Jesus, here I am. I don't really know what to do because I don't know much of Your Word or how I am supposed to talk to You but I would like for You to come into my heart and be my Lord. I know that I need You but I just don't need You, I deeply desire You. I want to be Your friend and walk with You and whether I live or I die today, I am placing my life in Your hands. Please help me. Please save me."

He said,

"I heard my mother begin to sing this song that she taught me when I was a boy. I knew she was singing through her tears. Something inside me began to leap and inside my heart, I joined her and in my heart we sang together. I felt like I was standing before God's throne, there was so much beauty and joy in my heart." He then noticed that his mom had stopped singing and called to his father Jose. She yelled, "Jose, come here! Look at the tears run down his cheeks! Our boy is still in there!" He said his dad told his mom, "Keep singing! We will stand before our God on behalf of our son until he comes back to us."

By this time, I wanted to burst out in tears. I noticed some of the men crying. All of us were on the edge of our seats. To look at this healthy middle-aged man you would never know he had gone through something so tragic and challenging. We listened intently to the rest of what he had to say and I sure was surprised at what came next. I expected him to say that his condition had turned around that very minute, but he didn't.

Pastor Jonathan said that it took many, many weeks before he "woke up." He said that while he lay there, hooked up to machines that were keeping him alive, his mother and father came faithfully to the hospital every day to pray for him and read God's Word to him.

"I enjoyed hearing about God. I had never felt like this before, even in the church I attended. I felt like I was hearing the pure Word of God and it washed me," he said.

Two things his parents did for him that he appreciated were that they brought in a CD player and would leave the Word or worship music playing, and they demanded that the hospital staff talk to him as though he was alive.

He went on,

"One day, I heard my parents in my room talking to my doctor. The doctor told them that it was time to make a decision because there was no sign that I would come out of the coma and even if I did, I may never be the son that they remembered. I knew I had to show this doctor I was still alive, so I prayed. I asked Jesus to help me speak to the doctor somehow. I listened to my parents insist that they would never agree to that because their son was alive and they saw signs of life."

He said the doctor took a deep breath and began to tell them what to expect in the days or weeks to come. He told them there was no hope. Pastor Jonathan said he told Jesus,

"The professionals caring for me have given up because of what they see. Lord help me to show them I am still alive."

He said he felt this strength well up inside of him and with everything in him, he lifted his hand. The doctor was on his way out the door when his mom cried out,

"Jesus! He is lifting his arm!"

The doctor turned around and walked back and then explained it was just a reflex. He said he heard a voice yell,

"No!"

And realized it was his voice. What could his doctor say now? He said the room came alive with praise and the doctor called in nurses and ordered a battery of tests to be done on him.

"It was still a slow process and many more weeks passed before I would open my eyes and begin signaling. I had to learn how to walk and speak again."

He looked at all of us as we were hanging on every word he said and he asked,

"Do you know how humiliating it is to not even be able to go to the bathroom on your own but have to be changed like you're a child? Do you have any idea how it feels to know that you're alive but almost everyone else thinks you're dead? Imagine how frightening it was for me. Although it was humiliating, I appreciated how well I was cared for. I also learned something about myself. I learned that before my accident I had become very prideful. Going through this ordeal, I felt that pride being destroyed inside me and being replaced by humility."

He paused again and said,

"I felt so alone at times. There were times I felt like giving up. There were even times I wanted to give up on God. I felt God was not moving fast enough to bring me out of my situation."

He looked around the room and said,

"Just like many of you."

My head fell and I could no longer hold back the tears. I heard him say,

"There are some of you who are innocent and did not commit the crimes that you stand accused of but no one is hearing you. You want to give up. You keep questioning God as to why this is happening to you and asking God why you deserve this. Maybe it's time to change your line of questioning. Ask God to show you what you are here for. Ask Him to reveal Himself to you. Your life has a greater purpose than what you see."

I knew God was talking to me through this man. God had my full attention and I was listening.

He told us that the first thing he did when he came out of the coma was open his Bible and look up everything he could about salvation. He realized that his church had taught him everything but the right thing and that he almost lost his soul because of it.

"As I made a full recovery, I got to know Jesus for real. I invited Him into my heart and believed that God raised Him from the dead. I got out of my hospital bed, got down on my knees, and began to cry for God to change me. I asked God to make me the man that I was meant to be, to help me be pure."

Pastor Jonathan then said,

"It is a lie from hell that tells men that because we are men, we can't live a pure life if we are not married."

Some of the men laughed. He looked at them and asked why they thought that was funny. One of the men said,

"Because chasing women is what we do."

More laughter!

Pastor Jonathan asked him how many children he had. This man then, got very serious. He said he had eight children. Pastor Jonathan asked him how many different women he has children by. He said three. Pastor Jonathan looked at him and said,

"Brother, I'm going to say this with all the love in me, but the number of babies that you make does not make you a man. While you are sitting here in prison, who is taking care of your children? When you get out of prison, how many hours are you going to have to work to pay for all of those children and how much of your time will you give them?"

The man got visibly angrier and angrier, but sat quietly.

Pastor Jonathan went on to say,

"We as men have bought into the hype that we need sex to make us men. Many men believe that the more women they have and the nastier they are, the more manly they are. If you want to serve God, you have got to be holy. God said that we are to be holy like He is holy."

One of the brothers raised his hand and asked how to do that. Many of us sat there nodding our heads in interest. He explained,

"We were made in the image of God and there is no filthiness in Him. Once we ask Jesus into our hearts, we have a holy and perfect King living inside of us. If we give Him the opportunity to show us how powerful He is and surrender to Him, we can be free from sins that we have struggled with. Salvation through Jesus Christ is the foundation of Christianity: deliverance and abiding in Him is how we grow in our salvation and walking in holiness will help us keep our deliverance."

He said,

"Deliverance is allowing the Holy Spirit to pull up the weeds of sin in our life, such as perversion and lying, or whatever sin we struggle with, and planting seeds of righteousness in their place. If you have a garden and there are weeds growing, they cannot just be mowed over because they will just keep growing back. Weeds have to be pulled out at the root so that the beauty of what should be growing can be healthy. This is what the Holy Spirit does when we allow Him to do so. He pulls the sin out at the root and replaces it with His beauty! Some of you are failing in holiness because you are not allowing God to process you in deliverance."

He continued teaching us,

"The more I stay in the presence of God through prayer, the Word and fasting, the less I desire sin and when I do fail, I am brokenhearted and quick to repent. I struggled with sexual sin because my flesh enjoyed it. The more I developed a relationship with the Lord, the less I wanted to sin against Him and I desired more of the holiness of God. The things that we know are sinful but that we enjoy doing are what God wants to take out of us right now. We have to first be saved and then be honest enough to look at the sin and confront it. Even if you are not quite ready to let it go, tell that to God. Tell Him the fulfillment it gives you then ask God to get you to a point where you hate it. That is how I approach God because He already knows what's in our hearts. Nothing hides from Him."

The service was quickly drawing to a close. Pastor Jonathan ended it by asking,

"Who would like to give their hearts to Jesus? The next breath is not promised, and you need to make a decision."

Hands went up all over, but I was still undecided so there I sat and lowered my head. Even though I felt God speaking to me, something held me back.

I got back to my cell and Gabe asked how service was. I told him,

"I really enjoyed it, but I'm still not sure about Jesus. I have lived my whole life in fear of what you call the supernatural realm, that's where Jesus lives."

Gabe said,

"Peter, you remind me so much of another man named Peter. He said he wanted to follow Jesus and walk on the water but when he conquered his fear and stepped out of the boat, he realized he was out of the safety of the boat and in the midst of a turbulent wind. Instead of keeping his eyes on Jesus, he looked at the storm and became filled with fear. That's when he began to sink but because Jesus loved him so much, he came to Peter's rescue and kept him from going under. Now does that sound like a God that you should be afraid of?"

He looked me in the eyes and asked,

"Peter, what is keeping you from getting out of the boat and trusting a God who spoke so lovingly to you tonight? And by the way, Jesus is everywhere. He is the creator of heaven AND earth. He cannot be contained in one realm."

They called for lights out and I found myself kneeling down beside my cot. I thought about everything that Gabe told me and everything I had learned from Pastor Jonathan. I found myself crying, asking God to come into my troubled heart. I talked to God all night long and poured my heart out to Him. I repented for my stubbornness and even told Him that I didn't want a jailhouse conversion but I wanted Him for real. When I opened my eyes, the sun was up. I felt like a new man, I guess because I was. I dried my eyes and looked over at the desk, excited to tell Gabe. He wasn't there.

I thought that maybe his lawyer had come to see him and in the state I was in I didn't hear him leave. I went over to the desk and all his belongings were gone except a note addressed to me. It said,

"Peter, keep pressing forward in the things of God and remember He is always there for you. Your friend, Gabriel."

Was my friend gone without me knowing it? How did I not hear him leave, and why would he leave without saying goodbye? I sat on my cot wondering where he was, but I felt so much peace that I eagerly opened up the Bible that was given to me at service last night. I was still a little intimidated by the length of this book but said,

"Well, I guess I'll start at the beginning. Genesis chapter one........"

New Beginnings

While I sat on my cot, my "favorite" officer, Terror, walked past my cell and I called out to him. He actually stopped and asked what I wanted. I asked him where my cellie was. He laughed and said,

"What cellie? You haven't had a cellie since you left the hole. What do you need, some meds or something? Are you hallucinating again?"

He laughed a huge belly laugh. I said,

"My cellie's name is Gabe. Did he go to court or something?"

He sarcastically replied,

"James, quit making up imaginary friends before you have to go see the shrink!"

He shook his head at me and walked away calling me an idiot. Again I sat down. Was this guy messing with me? I had been talking to Gabe for seven days. I think he's the idiot! Later in the day I asked another officer about Gabe and was baffled when he told me the same thing that Terror told me. No one had been assigned to my cell since I left the hole but someone was coming in a day or two.

My first question was:

"Am I losing my mind?"

The next question was:

"Did I dream all of that?"

The answer to the first question was, *perhaps*. The answer to the second question was, *it couldn't have all been a dream*. I just didn't believe I was dreaming everything because it was all too real. There was no way Gabe was just a figment of my imagination. He taught me so much, and knew so much about me. I felt that I knew who I could talk to about this: Pastor Jonathan.

When Monday night rolled around, I asked him if I could speak with him privately when service is over. He said sure. Service was another incredible move of God and I felt like I had been washed with the purest of water. My heart felt lifted and I also felt more encouraged. The teaching was from John the 15th chapter which had to do with abiding in Christ. Pastor Jonathan explained that this is how we grow in the things of God and this is also how we keep our deliverance. He said that at salvation, Christ comes to live in us but when we abide in Him, that's us living in Him. I loved this man's services because he was so simple yet so effective.

As promised, Pastor Jonathan pulled me to the side after service and asked,

"What's up?"

I started off with telling him that he may think I'm crazy when I say this and he retorted with:

"Try me!"

I began to tell him about my cellie, Gabe and all of the things that he taught me and how Gabe was always busy at our desk writing.

"Nothing strange there," he said.

"I haven't gotten to the strange part. Two officers told me that I hadn't had a cellmate since I got out of the hole. Am I crazy, because I know that there was a man in my cell talking to me and teaching me things about myself and about God? He even told me to come to your service and stay connected to you."

Pastor Jonathan laughed so hard that he had tears in his eyes. He collected himself and apologized.

"I wasn't laughing at you. I was laughing because now I know that you were the one God had been speaking to me about in my times of prayer."

I looked at him like he was nuts. Because I was so new at this Christian stuff, it was difficult for me to believe that God spoke to people like that. Of course I know now that our Father speaks to us in different ways. Sometimes He may speak to us with a still, soft voice, sometimes He will speak through His Word. He may even speak to us through other people or show us things through dreams and visions.

Pastor Jonathan said,

"God spoke to me about a young man that I would meet and mentor. The Lord also told me that you have many questions, some I may answer, and others He Himself will answer directly. God has you on a fast track because there is so much you need to learn so quickly, but He will talk to you directly about many things."

All he would say about Gabe is that he didn't believe I was crazy and that the Holy Spirit would show me about that in His time.

The officer came to get us and I walked out of there feeling a combination of confusion, anger and frustration. I felt like my question had been answered with riddles but I knew beyond the shadow of a doubt that I was not crazy. I felt like I needed to trust what I experienced. And, if Gabe didn't exist, who snuck into my cell and left me that note?

When I got back to my cell, I grabbed the note and analyzed it. I said to myself,

"Dreams don't write letters and leave them for people."

I know Gabe was real. I laid down on my bed and went over all the things he revealed to me, things I never shared with anyone. I couldn't help but smile. I said to God,

"You showed up when I needed You in the woods that night before I took my life and I believe that somehow, through my friend Gabe, You showed up again. God, I know that You are real and I want You to know that not only do You have my full attention but You have my heart. I am following You!"

As I lay there on my bed my mind went immediately to my troubled family. I began to cry out and plead with God to go to them and save them. I asked Him to heal my dad's heart and to stop him from running. I stopped at that and said,

"God, I really do love my dad and I forgive him for the hurt he caused me. I understand now that he just doesn't know how to love and that he is afraid. Thank You for my father that loved me enough to protect me and keep my life safe."

I could feel a new sense of forgiveness, although I was still sad that my parents hadn't come to see me. I didn't even know where they were because their letters were beginning to come back to me. I said,

"God, it's up to You."

Then a heartbreaking sadness washed over me and I felt a grief in me like never before. I was now coming face to face with the loss of my friends. I remembered seeing them covered in blood, beyond help.

"God, where did their souls end up? Oh my God, my friends! They were like my brothers."

I balled up in a fetal position and I cried like I never have before.

I felt so much loss. My freedom had been taken away. My family was, only God knows where, and my friends were gone. I kept thinking to myself,

"How could anyone hurt those guys? Had they done something wrong and this was revenge? Who did this to them?"

Then it hit me like a ton of bricks. Had I been there just minutes earlier, I could have been murdered. The same went for my brother, but he had been grounded. I could've lost him too! I thought about this over and over again.

"God it could have been me and I would have never had this opportunity to meet You. Or I could be grieving the loss of my kid brother."

This was a thought that I held onto throughout my time in prison. When I felt anger and wanted to just shake my fist at God for letting me be here I would come back to this thought: it could've been me.

When I went back to that day, I couldn't help but wonder was it God that had me stop by my workplace and help out? Did He tell my mother to not allow my brother to go because he didn't do his chores? I finally concluded in my heart that the answer was "yes." It had to have been God. The other thing I knew was that while I was standing accused of this crime, someone was out there allowing me to pay for what they did.

"God, who! Who did this?"

As the weeks went by my frustration grew. My attorney said that he was preparing for my trial and that it didn't look good. This pretty much became the norm from him. The only thing I looked forward to was church and seeing Pastor Jonathan.

This week he taught from Ephesians 6, about the Armor of God. I had never in my life heard of such things. As I went over my notes from the service I turned the page and found the one thing that stung me. I had circled the sentence: You are not fighting against flesh and blood. You are fighting against demons!

"God, what does this even mean?" I thought. "There is so much I don't understand. I am not fighting against people, but demons? That must mean that whoever did this to my friends is demon-possessed and the person is not my enemy, but whatever is in them is."

I had to wrap my mind around this. It was difficult to do! All I knew for sure is that someone had killed them. How was I supposed to excuse this person and blame it on some boogey man?

"God, how do I do this? How do I see this as truth?"

All at once, I felt anger again. All I could ask God was,

"HOW? How do I see past this person, whoever they are?"

I wanted to scream at God! I wanted to yell,

"WHAT IS THIS ALL ABOUT?"

I said,

"God, You let me come here. You let me take the blame for a crime I didn't commit, and now You're telling me that I can't even be angry at the person who did this?"

I put my Bible down because I had had enough for one night. Things were beginning to not make any sense and I felt lost again. My only prayer before I closed my eyes was,

"God please help me."

I drifted off to sleep. A dream filled sleep, sweet, sweet dreams.

In my dream, I was in another place, with no cell holding me and no prison bars. I walked around looking, enjoying the sun, and breathing in the fresh air. I kept walking, feeling like I was being led. As I rounded the corner there was a young man lying on the ground, bruised and beaten. I could tell he was weak. When I approached him to try to help him he turned toward me. It was me! I was standing there looking at myself. Then I realized he was not looking at me at all. He was looking past me, at someone else. I couldn't see the other man's face but he was dressed in what appeared to be a robe and I saw a sword hanging at his side. This man was so bright, and I felt like I knew him even though I could not see his face.

I asked,

"Who are you?"

He said,

"I AM."

When He said those words, I fell face first to the ground. I felt Him pick me up and as I turned to see the other me, I was gone. He carried me to another place and sat me down. I heard Him say,

"Peter, I have brought you to this place for a particular reason. I will use you for My glory to do many things. I am changing the way you think, the way you believe and I am even going to change the way that you love. You don't need to understand everything right now. You only have to keep your eyes trained on me. Do not worry about your current situation and do not worry about your family. One day at a time, Peter. I have all things in My hands. Stand, Peter, and be strong in Me!"

As soon as He said,

"Be strong in Me,"

I felt a strength like I had never felt. I looked at my hands and saw a light enveloping them that was so bright! When I looked to my right I saw myself again. I was surrounded by familiar creatures, creatures that I have seen in my nightmares all my life. They were trying to bite and curse me, but they didn't touch me. I realized that I was wearing armor that they could not penetrate. I kept repeating,

> *"Finally, my brethren, be strong in the Lord, and in the power of his might. Put on the whole armour of God, that ye may be able to stand against the wiles of the devil. For we wrestle not against flesh and blood, but against principalities, against powers, against the rulers of the darkness of this world, against spiritual wickedness in high places."* – Ephesians 6:10-12

I watched the "other me" speak this with boldness and I also watched the demons that surrounded me shudder in fear as though they were exposed! Then I heard myself say again,

"BE STRONG IN THE LORD AND IN THE POWER OF HIS MIGHT."

I woke up feeling different. I felt strong, but not an earthly kind of strong. I felt humbled and, through this humility, I felt strength. I immediately grabbed my Bible and turned to Ephesians 6. I found verse 10 and kept reading it over and over again. Finally, I focused on the words,

"BE STRONG IN THE LORD."

I felt as though I was releasing myself. I had an understanding that I cannot fight this in my strength, I cannot understand this with my mind, and I have to let God grant me His wisdom, knowledge, and love. I began to pray for just that. I wanted to see how God sees and I wanted to know what He wanted me to know. I even asked Him to help me to love the way He loves and to forgive the way He forgives.

As I sat on my bed I realized that our relationship with God is like our earthly relationships with each other. Sometimes they are "up." Sometimes they are "down." It is not because God is unbalanced because He never changes. The reason why we feel these ranges of emotions, even with Him, is because we tend to be emotional beings, and sometimes we even get mad at God. The difference with God is that He stays the same. He just loves. We do wrong and He responds in love. We get mad at Him and He just keeps loving. We don't obey sometimes but He continues to love. Even in His judgment He loves.

I repented to God for being angry with Him and asked Him to fill me with His love so that I forgive quickly. All I wanted was to hold on to that moment. I felt things changing in me for the better. I became hungry for His Word because I could feel His presence whenever I read it. I also knew that the more I read it, the more I was going to learn about this God that had saved me, changed me, and was now my friend.

Who Am I?

As I was spending time with God one day I came across this passage in the Scripture from Jeremiah 1:5 which says,

> *"Before I formed thee in the belly I knew thee; and before thou camest forth out of the womb I sanctified thee, and I ordained thee a prophet unto the nations."*

I was focused on the fact that it said that God knew me before I was in my moms' womb. I pondered that for a few minutes. If God knew me before I was conceived then doesn't that mean I existed in Him before I came into this earth? I went to Psalm 51:5;

> *"Behold, I was shapen in iniquity; and in sin did my mother conceive me."*

I began to understand through these 2 passages that because I existed in eternity with God before I came into this world, and before I was touched by the sin of this world, God had His hand on me first. Because God had His hand on me before Satan, I had to accept Jesus as Savior, then I had to find out who I am in Christ. I know that I am no longer a sinner because I have accepted Jesus as my Savior but having first come into this sinful world I learned sin first. Now I have to learn everything anew. I have to let Him show me how I am truly meant to function in Him.

I dug deeper and went to the beginning. I went to Genesis chapter 1. I never realized the power we have in our mouths until I read this again. God spoke the world into existence and He made us in His image. What a heavy thought to know that death and life are in the power of the tongue (Proverbs 18:21)!

I got to chapter 2 of Genesis and read that God formed Adam after He formed creation. He is very serious about us not trying to steal His glory! He gave Adam the charge to name everything and I remembered talking about this in service. A brother said that God showed him that there is so much power in our words that the animals' names have stuck to this day!

"Deep! Thanks for that revelation, brother!!"

I went on reading about how God told Adam that he could eat of everything in the Garden of Eden but the tree of the knowledge of good and evil. I read His next words very carefully. It said in verse 17,

> *"For in the day that thou eatest thereof thou shalt surely die."*

Adam did eat from that tree and the consequences for his disobedience were severe.

This goes to show that God knows everything we are going to do even before we do it. No, He is not a fortune teller. He is God. He is the creator. Think of Him this way. If I lay down designs for a building and then build it, I am birthing my creation and, because it is mine, I know everything about it. I know where the outlets are. I know the view from each window because I designed each window in its space. I even know what it would take to make it fall and so I put into it the strength to stand. I know everything about it and because I am the creator, if anyone has questions, they come to me and I teach them about it.

God is our creator and, because He designed us, He knows the things we are going to do in our lives. Nothing surprises Him or catches Him off guard. That's why He told Adam "WHEN you do this, you will die." Sometimes death doesn't mean physical death. There is such a thing as spiritual death, that is to say separation from God. It doesn't mean that God left because He said He would always be with us, more that sin gets between us and Him. What a frightening place to be in!

So God knew Adam was going to disobey Him. In Genesis chapter 3 this happens. I read this and thought,

"ADAM, HOW COULD YOU?"

Then I looked at my own life and thought,

"PETER, HOW COULD YOU?"

I could not judge Adam because I thought about how imperfect I am. Adam and Eve entertained Satan in the form of a serpent. The Bible says that the serpent was more subtle (or cunning) than any beast of the field which the Lord God had made. It was no wonder that Satan liked the form of the serpent!

Because they entertained wickedness by putting more weight in what the serpent said to them than God they fell into sin or death. Eve first ate, then she handed the fruit to her husband (sidebar: whenever I heard this story as a little boy, I was always told it was an apple. Ahhh, reading this for myself, I saw that it doesn't say what kind of fruit, so where did that come from?) As I read this I noticed that nothing happened when Eve ate and then handed it to Adam. When Adam ate, the bottom fell out! The world as they would know it changed.

God let me see that as a man, I am certainly not better than a woman but there is an authority inside of me. I am headship in this earth and God wants to use me to speak things into existence and to also safeguard the things I love the most against the enemy. I knew I had to learn how to pray and I had to learn the nature of how to exercise my authority! God, in His mercy, also let me realize this from this passage. I went back to the word "subtle" (verse 1) and studied its meaning. It means "cunning" or "crafty." Something was opening up in my understanding about this. God was connecting the dots of this word for me and how Satan deceived Adam and Eve. I looked again at the word "CRAFTY" or "CRAFT" as in "WITCHCRAFT!" I yelled,

"That's it! My family has been involved with witchcraft for generations and Satan has deceived them."

I knew how to pray for my family now, to pray against deception. I dropped to my knees and prayed for my loved ones. I called each by their names on both sides of my family. I prayed for those related to me that I didn't know. I asked God to remove deception from their minds, hearts, souls, and even their eyes. I prayed that God would reveal His truth to them and lead them to salvation. I prayed for hours for them and I believed God was doing it as I released the words. I was praying in agreement with His Word and so I knew it was being done.

There is so much power in our words that we must use them wisely. Take for instance Balaam in Numbers chapter 22. He was sent for by Balak to curse the people of Israel. God intervened on behalf of Israel and told him he was not to curse the people because they were blessed. In other words, if Balaam had spoken a word against Israel, he would have surely been an enemy of God because you cannot curse what God has blessed. He warned him,

"DON'T DO IT! Do not be in agreement with what is against Me."

We must use our words wisely.

In John chapter 11 verse 4, Jesus has been sent word that His friend Lazarus was sick and He should come quickly. Instead Jesus says,

> *"This sickness is not unto death, but for the glory of God, that the Son of God might be glorified thereby."*

God pointed out to me the first two words He said,

"This sickness."

Jesus used His words wisely by not referring to it as Lazarus' sickness because to do such a thing would give the spirit of sickness ownership over Lazarus and you cannot curse what God has blessed.

My faith in God was growing by leaps and bounds. Every time I prayed for my family I ended with,

"God, thank You for saving them, freeing them, delivering them and setting them in proper order according to Your Word, in Jesus' name."

I knew through faith that every time I prayed for them that God was getting closer. I may not see what is happening behind the scenes but I knew God was there and He was honoring my prayers.

One day, while I prayed, God said something to me that rather upset me. I heard Him say, "What about the person who murdered your friends? Have you prayed for him today?" I immediately felt a rush of anger! I was mad and I wanted to stay mad! I didn't want to hear God say anything so loving about an absolute monster. I wanted whoever had committed this crime that I was paying for to suffer. My next thought was, "Sure I'll pray for the murderer. I'll pray that they suffer more than my buddies did in that field. How 'bout that?" I then felt in my heart,

"Would you care to be judged by the same words you want to release?"

I went from my knees to lying straight on the floor.

"God, how do I pray for someone that I feel so much hatred for?"

God then asked me,

"Peter, do you want to be forgiven?"

"Of course I do" I answered.

God said to me,

"Let me take the hatred out of you. Just give me permission to do it and mean it. I want you free so that when you stand in need of forgiveness, I can forgive you and not be limited by the murderous spirit in your heart."

When God used the word "murderous" to describe my heart I saw it. I felt that if I was locked in a room with whoever had murdered Tony and Sam, I would become a killer myself. Oh God, help!

My Mountain, Myself

I can truly say that the soul of a person can be compared to an onion. There's always a new layer that has to be peeled away. I saw my growth in faith and I was understanding God's Word more and more but my heart was in bad shape. I had to deal with me. Sometimes looking at yourself is the hardest thing to do but I was determined to win. God did not create any of us to walk in defeat. He created us to win so that we can help others in their weaknesses. I got in His Word and began to read every Scripture I could find about love. This was the area that needed to be dealt with in my heart. I wrote Scriptures out and hung them all over my cell. I was determined to bombard this hatred with the love of God and put it on the run!

I came to Mark 11 starting at verse 22 where Jesus was telling the disciples to have faith in God. He began teaching them that they could tell mountains to move if they had the faith to believe that they would move and not doubt it. I thought on that and said to myself,

"I'm faced with two mountains. One is this feeling in my heart for the person who killed Tony and Sam. The other is this lie that has taken my freedom away."

I realized that these two things went hand in hand. If I wanted to be freed and cleared of this crime that I had not committed I had to forgive.

Jesus went on to say, that whatever we desire, when we pray, we are to believe that we will receive it. He then says that when we pray we are to forgive everyone we have not forgiven. And there it was: the next thing He says is, if we don't forgive, He can't forgive us. That was what He spoke to me the other day! I knew the "Lord's Prayer" in Matthew 6 but I think I needed to see it from the perspective of the mountain. I need these mountains in my heart moved first so that this physical mountain (prison) could then be moved! I said,

"God I think I got it. Here it goes!"

I knelt on my knees and slowly spoke the words,

"I FORGIVE YOU! I don't know who you are or where you are but I am releasing you into God's hands."

I could feel resistance in me because I know God as a loving God and the last thing I wanted this person to have was God's love. Then I said,

"Lord, please teach me to forgive. I need my words, my mind and my heart to be in agreement with You. I'm going to keep speaking this until I mean it. I have to!"

I asked God to let His love erase hate in my heart. Even that was difficult to pray for and as I write this I cannot act like this was an easy thing. I will never try to come off like I am some super-Christian because I am not. Sometimes the process is difficult but if we want the freedom of God we have to stay in the process until we see change.

Every day I woke up telling myself,

"Forgive him. Release him."

Every night, before I lay down, I said,

"I forgive you."

I couldn't quite get the words "I love you" out but one thing at a time. I knew that I didn't want to go to sleep without allowing God to deal with my heart, not when He has exposed this truth to me and I see clearly.

One night I woke myself up punching my pillow. I realized that I was dreaming about being face to face with this person and it ended in a physical manifestation of me fighting. I cried out to God because I felt like I was not winning the battle over this thing. I was no longer even focusing on getting out of prison and being cleared of the charges. I was focused on my heart. I wanted to be free from the inside out.

I kept digging in and desiring complete forgiveness. The irony in this part of my story is that as I was tackling unforgiveness in my heart, God was sending men to me to pray for them, many of whom were then released from prison! At first I felt jealous. Why them and not me? Then I realized that God was giving me this honor and trusting me to pray for these men. I had the chance to lead many of them to Him and these men trust me. Who am I to be jealous because He was blessing them? Why would I be upset because He is answering my prayers? I knew I had a long way to go but I was willing to go. The joy I had praying and just listening to these brothers, sharing Scriptures with them and learning from them, was immense. I stopped praying for God to let me leave this place and I began praying for His will to be done in me and through me.

Our services continued to grow but we needed more than just a Monday service. We formed a prayer group that the prison officials allowed to come together three times a week. I was stunned at the favor God showed us. Someone went to one of the captains, who was also a Christian, and asked if we could begin a Bible study. He said he would talk to the warden and came back with a "yes." Thursday nights were now Bible study and we were even allowed to use a classroom. There were officers just down the hall and cameras in the room so that everything could be seen, but we didn't care. This was freedom for us.

On my night to share one of the officers came to tell me that there were some rough guys who were involved in gangs coming to the study. They did not want to allow them all to come but the ranking officer told them it would be all right. I wondered why he told me. Who am I that an officer would give me such a warning? Everyone piled in. There must have been at least 35 men, most of whom were regulars and some brand new. I shook off trying to figure out who was who because it was none of my business. We opened with prayer and then one of the brothers asked if he could share a song that he had written. As he sang it we could feel God's presence surrounding us. I opened my eyes and most of the men had their hands lifted to God. Some were crying and thanking Jesus. Others were just wondering what was happening.

When the song was over, we stood and clapped in encouragement to this brother who was growing so much in God. Him sharing that song and doing it in front of the crowd was a very different experience for him. He always made sure to be in the back of the room for services and never said anything. All I could think was "look at our Lord and what He is doing here."

I got up and moved to the front of the room. The atmosphere was incredible. God's love was everywhere. I explained to those who were new that what they had witnessed was God. I said, "Jesus died for us all so that even in prison we could be free. He loves us and He wants to share His love with everyone in the room." Walls were falling the more I spoke. I could see it. The hardened gang members were listening. God had their attention.

I had been reading about Joseph (beginning in Genesis 37). I shared with the men that I sometimes feel like Joseph and that his story had become very important to me. In prison, you don't share your crime or especially the fact that you have been wrongly accused so I told them that Joseph was special to me because he chose to grow while he was in prison. He was falsely accused but instead of defending himself, he let God reveal Himself to him and because of that God's favor went before Joseph.

Someone raised their hand and asked what "favor" meant. I said,

"Well, the best way I can describe it is being blessed by God even though we don't deserve it. Remember Brother Tommy who was part of our men's group? He was given a twenty year sentence and took responsibility for his crime. He served God wholeheartedly while in prison and led many to Christ. He always seemed happy, even to be locked up. I asked him one day why he smiled so much. He said, 'Because I'm free.' Two weeks ago, Tommy walked out of here after serving only eight years of his sentence. No one could understand, not even him. That to me is God's favor. I just got a letter from him and he has been given a good job and is knee deep in ministry. He is still serving God and said in his letter, 'Fight the good fight of faith whether you are incarcerated or whether you are on the outside. We are nothing without Him!'"

I could see the light bulbs turning on and smiles and "amens" filled the room. I continued on with Joseph. I didn't want to talk to them about his incarceration and how it was wrong, rather I talked to them about Joseph's relationship with his brothers. We read chapter thirty-seven. As one of the guys read this I watched the reaction in the room. It was hitting many of the men. When he finished reading my question to them was this: "How could his own flesh and blood hate him so much that they wanted him dead and how did Joseph forgive them?"

Some men squirmed in their seats. I went on to say,

"Joseph found out, like maybe some of you, that sometimes it is your very own family that has a death warrant out for you. Sometimes it is the ones who are supposed to love you the most, the ones you grew up with, who want to see you fail. Joseph shared his dreams with his brothers which made them even more jealous of him because he already had so much of their father's heart and now he's telling them that one day they would bow before him?"

I continued,

"Well, the wisdom of God says that you can't share everything with everyone but I wonder about two things. If they knew that selling Joseph into slavery would trigger the very events that they wanted to kill him over would they have still listened to their brother Reuben? Also, had Joseph not gone to prison, would he have learned the forgiveness of God the way he did?" I went on, "Something that I learned from Joseph's story is that because he was human, he probably had a lot of rage in him against his brothers for some time. They stripped him of everything and took his father away from him for many years."

I told the men,

"One thing is certain with Joseph, if he had not let God get his heart right, he would not have been the leader that he turned out to be. I believe that sometimes God removes us from what's familiar so He can rewire us. Joseph's brothers already hated him and were jealous of him so he would have had the warfare of that problem even if they hadn't sold him. He had to be moved away into safety so that God could deal with his heart and pour His love into him. When Joseph came face-to-face with his brothers again it was as the second-in-command of Egypt! His brothers had to bow before him and they didn't know who he was but Joseph knew them. When Joseph revealed to them who he was he didn't have them killed or thrown in prison. Joseph embraced them. He cried over them. He loved them and he forgave them. He had the power and authority for revenge and would not have been questioned. Instead, he did what Jesus did: he forgave and loved."

I looked at all of the men there one after the other and said,

"While God has you here, don't waste time holding onto grudges and hatred. God wants to do something in you and He wants to use you for His glory. How do you know that He will not send you into the very areas filled with people who hated you and use you to bring His salvation to them? Think about the people who have wronged you and ask yourself, have I released them yet? If the answer is 'no,' get busy asking God to help you. Holding onto such things only hurts you! God wants us free even in prison!"

Our time was up and we ended with the invitation for salvation. There were five brothers who raised their hand and prayed with me. As they asked Christ into their hearts I saw a softness overtake them. Before they knew it there were tears falling to the floor.

We all expressed our love for them and encouraged them to keep coming. Everyone began to leave. The officer who gave me the warning had slipped into the room while we prayed. No one saw him. When everyone left, he said to me as he pointed,

"You see those three men? Those are three of the hardest gang members in here and those two hugging belong to rival gangs. What in the world happened in here tonight?"

I said simply,

"God happened."

As I watched these three men talk and shake hands with each other I thought about something that Pastor Jonathan had prayed for months ago. He prayed,

"God ignite the fire for revival in this place!"

Was this the beginning of what he prayed for? I couldn't help but think that it was.

When my new cellie, Ty, went to sleep I knelt before God. I couldn't comprehend how such a holy God would allow me to stand before His people to do anything. I thanked Him for that and I thanked Him for the souls that were saved. Then I thanked Him for being in this place. I said,

"God, I don't know if I would have met You if I hadn't come here. I certainly would not have met these men who have become my brothers. God You have a reason for everything and tonight I can say I forgive him. I forgive him because he must be living in his own personal hell right now. Although I am here because of him, I'm free because I have You. Lord, Joseph forgave his own family who had murder in their hearts against him. Jesus You keep forgiving screw ups like me. Who am I to not forgive? God, wherever he is and whoever he is, don't just bring him to justice, bring him to You. I will remain here for as long as You keep me here but my life is tied to You. I love You Lord."

I read a couple chapters in Psalms and I went to sleep, a peaceful sleep.

The next morning as we got ready for work an officer came to the cell and told me the captain wanted to see me. My cellmate and I looked at each other. I followed the officer over to the captains' office where he sat waiting for me. He invited me to sit down and asked me if I wanted a job. I said,

"I already have one sir."

He said,

"I heard you like to pray."

I had no idea where this was going but I answered that I did. He said he wanted to try me out in a new area and told me if I didn't like it I could move back to my old job.

"Okay, what is it?"

He said,

"Come with me."

We walked into an area of the prison that I had never been in before and I'm thankful that I hadn't. We were in the infirmary. He told me to come over and get a gown, gloves and a mask, which I did and we were buzzed through another door. He looked at me and said,

"Since you like to pray for people, I thought this would be a good area for you to work in. Now, you are not here only to pray for them. You're here to pray as you work."

He introduced me to the doctor in charge and told him to show me what he wanted me to do. I didn't know what to say other than, to thank him. The Captain nodded to me and left.

The doctor introduced himself as Doctor Harrison and I told him my name. He said,

"Well, Mr. James, let's get you busy. Over in that area is a bucket and mop. Are you good at cleaning?"

I said,

"Yes sir."

He looked at me with a scowl. I said,

"I mean, yes Doctor."

I didn't know what was going on or why I was moved over here but I knew that God had me on assignment for something. I grabbed the mop and bucket and I mopped joyfully and quietly prayed for His healing to spread throughout this place and for everyone in here to get the best medical attention that they could get. I thanked God for His favor. The officers were either watching me, or someone was talking to them about me. My mind was made up that I was going to let God's light shine through me no matter what. I wanted to be an example of Him. Hmm, you truly never know who is watching you, do you?

Have You Considered My Servant?

While I loved my new job because it gave me the opportunity to talk to people and lead some to Christ that wanted to know Him and to encourage others, the doctor, on the other hand, ran the place like a drill sergeant. He was cold to everyone and behaved as though he hated being there. There were a couple of times he threw things at me and when they made a mess, of course my duty was to clean it up. I said,

"God this has to be why You moved me here. Sick people need compassion and this cold hearted man needs You."

I targeted him in prayer and believe me I was tested over and over again. He was one tough nut!

Over the intercom, the doctor was told that my attorney was there and an officer was on the way to escort me to see him. As usual, I said goodbye and as usual, he didn't acknowledge that

I was even alive. A couple of the nurses smiled and waved and then got back to work. They were nice people. One of them was older than my mom and she had a heart of gold. She loved her work and did it with excellence.

I got to the meeting room and had already asked God to prepare me for whatever was to happen. We got our pleasantries out of the way and he told me that there had been a number of favorable developments in my case. I refused to let my eyes show any glimmer of hope, though. He said,

"The bad news is that with every development the DA is moving to have it stricken, and the judge keeps siding with them."

He looked at me again and said,

"Peter, hear me good. They are coming after you with everything they have and they are seeking the death penalty. They are willing to accept a guilty plea in exchange for a life sentence. Unless you plead guilty, I may not be able to save you. Do you understand me? You are facing death."

I looked at him and said,

"Why should I be responsible for what I did not do? I can't accept their plea bargain."

He lowered his head.

"I don't know if it is your age keeping you from understanding or stubbornness."

I told him,

"It's my innocence."

He said that the atmosphere of the town was still against me and that they wanted this to come to a close quickly. In other words, you don't have any friends there so you better hope you have some friends upstairs with the Big Guy. I smiled.

He asked me how I was doing after hearing that. I said,

"Whatever God's will is will be done, no matter who is against me. God does not punish those who are not guilty."

At that he looked at me and asked,

"You don't feel like you are being punished being in this prison?"

My answer surprised even me.

"I am on assignment and this will end when God is ready for it to end."

He told me that it sounds almost like I was giving up. I said,

"You couldn't be further from the truth."

Our meeting ended with the usual, him saying he is still fighting for me and me telling him okay. The officer came to get me and I returned to my cell. For the first time, I wasn't angry or scared after meeting with him. I just wanted to get back to God.

That evening at dinner I couldn't imagine what was about to happen. Two of the brothers from service got into an argument and I went over to talk to them quietly. All of a sudden, one of them hit me and knocked me out! I mean, I was out! When I came to, I looked up and realized that I was on the floor. There were officers everywhere and the two men who were arguing were now in a full blown fight. It was heartbreaking to see brothers who have prayed together fighting. I could see that the officer we call Terror was on his way. Those two men were grabbed by officers, I was grabbed by a grinning Terror and all three of us were thrown in the hole.

I could hear men saying,

"He wasn't fighting. He was trying to break it up."

This was met with,

"You wanna go too?"

I shook my head all the way there thinking,

"Man, Kevin has quite a left hook."

Terror was so happy for this trouble he was almost floating on air. I felt like he especially had it in for me. There I was, again. I said to myself,

"God, why does Terror treat us like this? Why is he so angry and what happened just now? Why am I back in here for trying to do the right thing?"

As I talked to God and then became quiet, I heard this:

"His name is Officer Terrie and no matter how he behaves, he is the authority. All authority comes from Me. Respect it. As for you, you are here for trying to help, understand that the rules outside do not apply in here. You tried to do a good thing but you, son, overstepped your authority. It is the responsibility of the officers to handle disputes."

Although God spoke strongly to me I agreed and repented. I was just glad that I could hear Him so clearly, even if it wasn't to baby me.

After a couple of hours, the captain came in to see me. He asked what had happened and I told him,

"I heard them arguing and I wrongly tried to step in instead of allowing the officers to handle it. I was disappointed that brothers were fighting and I didn't want them to get in trouble, but I realize now that I am not the authority here and I should have stayed in my seat."

He looked at me and said,

"Let's go."

He believed me! As we left, Terror (I mean Officer Terrie) stood there with rage in his face. I stopped in front of him and apologized for not following the rules and told him that I hope no one was hurt. He said nothing and we left. He had another officer take me to my cell where I immediately thanked God for His intervention.

I sat on my bed and my friend Ty, asked me what had happened. I told him and he said,

"Unheard of!"

I said,

"What's unheard of?"

He said that even though I tried to stop a fight I broke the rule and I am out of the hole in a matter of hours. I said,

"You know what, I was wrong and God got me straight. I repented and apologized to Officer Terrie."

He immediately asked,

"Who?"

I said,

"Officer Terrie. The one who is called Terror, his name is Officer Terrie."

He shot me a look and said,

"Whatever man. Goodnight."

Before the lights went out, I decided to do something different. I just let my Bible fall open to see what would happen. It opened to Jeremiah chapter 32 where I saw these words highlighted at verse 27:

> *"Behold, I am the Lord, the God of all flesh: is there any thing too hard for Me?"*

All I could do was smile and then the lights went out. Despite the bad news from my attorney, being punched in the face and thrown in the hole, I took a deep breath, said,

"Thank You Lord."

And drifted off to sleep.

T.G.I.M.

Thank Goodness It's Monday

Monday rolled around and once I was done with work, I went back to my cell and just thought. I thought about my family and about my friends. I thought about how I had been in this stinking place for so long. Everything seemed so bad but I didn't feel sadness. I said,

"God, my family is in Your hands. I also know that You will bring the person or people who killed my friends to justice. Lord, I forgive and release this to You also. I pray that no matter what You have to do, save whoever did this."

I felt a tear roll down my cheek and a stirring in my heart. I really wanted them saved because they needed Jesus just like I did. Wow! I really felt my heart crying out for them. Then I thanked God for allowing me to come here to meet Him and Gabe and Pastor Jonathan. I prayed for Officer Terrie and for his salvation.

I just had this understanding that these officers and administrators come in to a place like this where there is such a concentration of the demonic, and if they don't know Christ, they have nothing in them to fight this. They take on the atmosphere of this place. Then they go home and behave more and more out of character and don't even know why. They come back the next day and it starts all over again. I knew I needed to pray for the staff with purpose. There are those who know Christ and I thank God for them but those who don't know Him need Him whether they know it or not.

I lined up for church once the call was made and was excited to see Pastor Jonathan. I was surprised to see that he had brought in a team of people with him. There was a man who looked to be in his thirties, a woman whom I found out was his wife and a young woman. She was beautiful. She looked my age and didn't have an ounce of makeup on but she didn't need it. Her jet black, curly hair was pulled back into a ponytail and she dressed very simply. She had on a shirt that bore the word SERVANT in big letters and a Bible in the background. She looked exactly like Pastor Jonathan.

One of the guys noticed me staring at her and said, "That's Pastors' daughter Hadassah. You want me to introduce you to her? She's really nice." I said no and was embarrassed that I had been caught. I felt like my face was dark red and tried to busy myself with something else. I don't know what it was about her but I felt a connection to her. I remembered that name from reading the book of Esther in the Bible. What a beautiful name for a beautiful woman.

As everyone sat in their seats Michael was busy helping our guests with whatever they needed. I looked around to see if the two brothers that had been fighting had made it out of the hole yet but I didn't see them. Michael stood at the podium, welcomed everyone, and said that we need to keep two of the brothers who attended the service in prayer. He told us to call out what we all had in our heart to lift before God as we approached His throne and he began praying. I loved to hear this man pray! He was so genuine.

Immediately, one of the women began to sing in Spanish. It was her, Hadassah. I didn't understand a word she was singing, but I felt God. I looked around the room. There were men on their knees with their hands lifted, others so choked up that they were just staring past the ceiling and into the heavens. Then I heard another voice and a guitar. My God, what was happening in here tonight? This room, this prison, was being transformed into a sanctuary right before my eyes. I began to cry out for God to allow this to flow throughout this whole place and fell to my knees. Pastor Jonathan began to sing a familiar worship song and all of us sang along.

When I stood to my feet and opened my eyes I couldn't believe what I was looking at. Behind Pastor Jonathan and his guests there stood two angels! I could see them clearly. One angel had bright blond hair and the bluest eyes I've ever seen. The other angel was dark-skinned and his eyes were a soft brown. I felt great peace.

I wanted to look to see if anyone else saw them but I didn't want to break this vision. They were watching the worship taking place. I thought to myself that this is incredible that God is letting me see this. As the singing stopped we were still in God's presence and there was a stillness in the room. I concluded that the angels must travel with Pastor Jonathan. At once, as though they heard me, they trained their eyes on me and the blond-haired angel said,

"Peter, we are assigned to you. God deemed it time for you to see past the things in your life that have scared you and to see that He is with you. We are here because He sent us to you."

The other angel said,

"Peter, you will not always see us but God is always with you. You will receive a visit by the end of this week and you are to prepare your heart."

They were gone.

I felt someone tug on my shirt. I looked around. Everyone had been sitting down and was looking at me. Pastor Jonathan asked me if I had something I wanted to share. I said no and sat down. I looked at Hadassah, who was looking back at me. She gave me a beautiful smile and looked away. I thought my heart melted seeing her smile but then I went back to the angels. I looked around the room to see if I could see them but I didn't. I whispered,

"Thank You again Jesus."

And waited for the Word.

Pastor Jonathan got up and said,

"I am honored to introduce my daughter Hadassah to those of you who don't know her. I am equally honored that my baby girl will bring the Word of God tonight and I expect your full attention for the Word."

Everyone said,

"Amen."

She took the podium and thanked her father. I could see the love that they had for each other. At her age, she didn't seem to mind him calling her his baby girl. You could tell they were close.

Although she said that she felt led to speak to us from Proverbs 31 and the virtuous woman it was strange to me that she was speaking to men about this. She read from verses 10-31 and then looked around the room. She spoke with authority like her father. When she ministered, there was nothing delicate about this beautiful flower. She was standing in the authority of God and told us that if we were going to follow Christ in here we needed to make the decision to follow Him out there when we are free.

"Those of you who are not married yet and have a desire to, need to allow the Holy Spirit to purify you for your wives. Because you are men of God you should seek women of God. You should accept the best that God has to offer you in a mate because whoever you tie yourselves to will either add or subtract to your lives. A woman who is keeping herself for her husband will not allow herself to be tied to a filthy, perverted man."

Some of the brothers put their heads down and you could tell her words were hitting home.

She walked back and forth in full command of the congregation. She was beautiful to look at but now I was seeing past that. I was seeing her spirit. She loved God more than she even loved her father. I looked at Pastor Jonathan who was BEAMING with joy. I even saw tears in his eyes.

"A virtuous woman who is placed in your life by God is going to add to you and to whatever God has called you to do. Don't seek the lap of Delilah, but the woman who is of noble character and who is more than a pretty face. She will be worth more than rubies and that is how you are to treat her."

Many of the men were sitting at the edge of their seat listening to what God was instilling in our spirits. When she was done, she prayed for those of us who desire marriage when we leave prison. She prayed that we would wait for the woman God has for us. Then she prayed that those who were married even while they were incarcerated would be the man of God that their wives needed. She asked God to show us how to cover our wives with prayer, even those who were not married yet. Then she prayed that our wives would allow God to prepare them for their husbands and to wait for us.

This woman prayed with fire, well beyond her years. Those who were looking lustfully at her were pierced through the heart by the time service was over. I sat there and let it all pour over me. The worship, the angels, the Word: BEAUTIFUL. Then I wondered to myself, "who will this visitor be who will come see me? I only have my family, including my moms' parents and my attorney on my list, and I don't even know where my parents are. Well, we shall see."

The officers came to get us and called us pod by pod. Before they called mine Pastor Jonathan grabbed my hand and said,

"Come meet my family."

He introduced me to the man and woman who had helped in worship and I told him how much I loved hearing him play the guitar. I said,

"Hey, maybe one day you can teach me how to play."

He said,

"Peter, consider it done."

Then I turned and there she was. Pastor said,

"Peter, I want you to meet my baby girl, Hadassah."

She smiled as she looked at the floor. I could tell that she loved him calling her that. She looked up at me and said,

"Pleased to meet you, Brother Peter."

I told her how much I had gotten out of the Word and thanked her. The officer called my pod and as I walked away I turned to look at her one more time and I heard the Lord say,

"Your gift."

She smiled as though she heard it too and waved. God, was I embarrassed! I knew I was blushing.

I didn't quite know what those words meant. I just said,

"God, whatever gift You have for me, I accept it and ask that You prepare me for it. I also ask that You not let my mind get caught up in thinking about her. I need to keep my eyes on You."

Back in my cell, I talked to Ty about the service. He didn't go because he had not been feeling well. I asked him if he had been to the infirmary yet and He said no.

"What's going on?" I asked.

"I've been having horrible migraines for two days now, and today I threw up twice."

I asked him if I could pray for him and he welcomed it. I took him by the hand and thanked God for him. As I prayed I felt my hands become really hot, like fire. I laid my hands on his head and prayed for his healing in Jesus' name and I thanked God for it. Sweat poured from his forehead. When I felt like God was done, I thanked Him for hearing our prayers and for healing him and we both said "amen."

Something was different in me. I could feel it. I backed away from him and looked at my hands. They were burning red.

This had never happened before. Ty was sitting on the side of his bed, still with his eyes closed and still thanking God. He was soaked with sweat. We both laid down and when I looked at my hands again they were the same ole hands I remembered. I knew he had been healed, even if he didn't feel relief just yet. I knew God was healing him.

When we got up the next morning for devotions, he leaped off his cot and said,

"GOD I FEEL GOOD! I've suffered with migraines all my life. When they come on, I'm out of commission for sometimes weeks. I just learned to live with the pain, but now it's gone! I don't know why I believe they are not coming back but I do!"

We prayed together again and thanked God for his healing and asked God to order our day. We prayed for His blessing to be released throughout this prison and parted company until the evening.

Plea Deal

Today was Thursday, visiting day for my block. I remembered what the angels had said but kept my mind occupied with my duties at work. Around 4pm Officer Jones was standing in the door talking to the doctor and I was told I had a visitor. I thought,

"Well, here we go. God, You told me to be prepared."

Part of me believed it was probably Pastor Jonathan. Part of me hoped it was Hadassah. I shook it off and prepared myself for whatever he was going to tell me. Maybe he saw me staring at his daughter and was here to confront me.

When I walked into the visiting room I almost fell over! It was my dad!!! I rushed to the phone;

"Hi daddy."

I was surprised I called him that since I was a grown man but seeing him made me gush inside. My dad was here to see me after being ripped out of his home and out of his arms. I hadn't heard from him at all since I was arrested so this was truly a gift.

He looked like he had aged twenty years and had dark circles under his eyes. He finally spoke. I realized the shock of seeing his first-born in prison like this was horrible for him and there was nothing he could do. He asked me how I was and we got that conversation out of the way. The next thing he said to me was,

"You look different. I can't believe that you look happy in a place like this with two murder charges hanging over your head."

I said,

"Dad, let's talk about that later. How are you?"

He said,

"Well, I was forced into retirement because apparently the company I worked for thought it was bad for business to employ the father of a double murderer."

His words stung. He saw that I was hurt and apologized for lashing out.

"I have more bad news. Your grandmother Rosey passed away yesterday."

What a blow that was, but Grandma knew God, so I had peace about her passing. I asked about Granddad.

"He's going to be moving into a much smaller place and seems okay, although he misses her. He called your mom today and asked her if your grandma was at our house. When your mom told him that she had passed, he just said, oh yeah, that's right."

I knew in my heart it wasn't going to be long for Granddad. The two of them had been so close.

He looked at me with intensity and just blurted out,

"Why are you doing this?"

I asked,

"Doing what, Dad?"

He almost yelled,

"Why won't you just take the deal? Raph said they are still willing to accept it and said how unusual that is given how long it's been."

I told him,

"I couldn't take it because I didn't do it."

He responded with,

"At least you will get to live, even if it is in prison! Do you know what this is doing to all of us? Don't you understand that if they find you guilty you will eventually go to death row and wait for them to put you down like some dog? Peter, they will strap you to a bed and inject poison into your body to make your heart stop! Don't you get it? Take the deal!"

His words shook me and for the first time I saw clearly what could happen to me. If I'm convicted, they're going to kill me for something I didn't do. A fear wrapped itself around me. I opened my mouth to say,

"Ok Dad. Just tell the attorney to come see me."

But then I thought,

"If I take the deal, I'm admitting to murder and will always be labeled as such. At least if I stand in my conviction I will die saying to the end that I was innocent."

Then the words of one of my favorite Bible verses from Jeremiah 32:27 came back to me:

"Behold, I am the Lord, the God of all flesh: is there any thing too hard for me?"

I was standing at a crossroad. I either had to trust God, or be labeled a murderer and wait for my execution day.

"Dad I don't expect you to understand this, and I know you are worried about me, but I can't do that. I'm not trying to be stubborn. I didn't do this and I should not say I did something I did not do."

He let out a hard breath. I told him,

"I am a believer now."

He said,

"A believer in what, Peter?"

I replied,

"In Christ."

He rolled his eyes and said,

"You too?"

I looked at him and wondered what he meant. He continued his belittlement by saying,

"So you come to jail and get a jailhouse conversion and somebody's got you believing in fairytales? You really believe that something out there that freaks call 'God' is gonna get you out of this? You think He's going to wave His wand and the doors will magically open, Peter? This is real life and death, not make believe!"

I let him finish and then asked him why he believes Satan is real but can't believe that God is real? His mouth fell open. He said,

"Who told you that, your mother?"

I answered,

"Dad, I found all kinds of satanic stuff at the house one day. I know that you introduced Mom to the occult. If you can worship Satan, why can't you believe that God exists? Who do you think created Satan, or Lucifer as he was called in the beginning? Where did he come from, Dad?"

He snapped back,

"I don't believe in any of it! It's all nonsense and I'm not here to be converted. Peter, none of it is real. There was a time in my life when I was young and trying to be rebellious. That's where all of that stuff came from. I grew up and now you need to do the same."

I lovingly asked,

"Who have you been running from all of my life? Why did you move us from city to city, sometimes not even having a job in sight? You were afraid of something and that was your way of keeping us, me, safe."

I looked him in his eyes when I said "me."

"Do you know why I never allowed my parents around you without being there?" he asked.

I said,

"Tell me."

He was only willing to tell me parts of a truth by saying,

"My father was insane, and a violent drunk. I didn't want you to be around what I grew up with all my life."

I knew why my dad kept us on the run but he wasn't ready to deal with it. I knew that I was supposed to be a satanic sacrifice when I was born. I thought I would mellow the conversation and just thank him for keeping me safe.

"How are Mom and Brian?" I asked.

He told me,

"Well, they've been hit by the nutty fairy too, it seems. They claim to be Christians and your brother Brian is especially crazy with it! They go to some church all the time and carry their little Bibles. Brian has Scriptures all over his room, especially one that says, let me try to remember, something like: Is any thing too hard for the Lord?"

If I knew I wouldn't get thrown into the hole I woulda done a back flip! My mom and brother both Christians? I thought to myself:

"God You told me to put them in Your hands, and now I know they are." I asked,

"Why don't they write me? I would have loved to hear about their developing faith."

He said,

"I told them it wasn't a good idea for them to write because I didn't want them to hear about what it's like for you to be in prison. Your mom tries to smile but I still see her crying sometimes. Brian doesn't talk about any of it other than saying that God is going to bring you home."

He rolled his eyes again.

I said,

"Well, at least someone believes that I'll come home... I'm sorry Dad. I love you and I'm praying for you."

He responded,

"Peter, I don't believe in any of that stuff but if you do, you should pray they don't kill you."

I noticed the pentagram necklace that he always wore was absent.

"Dad, where's your necklace?"

He told me,

"Your mother came to me one day about that box from my dad and said she wanted to get rid of it. I agreed and gave her the necklace also. She threw everything in the garbage."

Again, I whispered,

"Lord, Thank You!"

Our visit time was almost over and I asked him for their new phone number and address. He was reluctant to give it to me but I promised him that I would not say anything about how tough prison is or has been and upset the household. He told me what it was and I memorized it as I could not write it down.

"Please tell everyone I love them. I'm sorry to hear about Grandma and that I can't be there for her funeral."

He promised he would. I said again that I loved him. He looked at me with tears in his eyes and said,

"I love you too, son."

He called me son again. I understood how Hadassah felt when her dad called her "Baby Girl."

It is Time

My attorney informed me that a trial date had been scheduled. When he told me this, my old familiar enemy, FEAR, hit me like a flood! I now had two choices. I could believe God, or I could believe that I was heading for the death chamber. I was looking at two paths and trying to decide which to take.

When I laid down that night it seemed like I was in an old place in my life. It had been some time since their last unwelcome visit, but here they were again, the familiar smells, sounds and torment. My enemy was fear and it was time for me to tackle it. I could hear demonic laughter and I heard one of them say they couldn't wait to see me take my last breath as they injected me with the poison to kill me. "You thought you could escape us? You were our sacrifice from the womb and now we will finally have your blood that is rightfully ours!" Over and over again, their words painted horrific scenes in my mind of what it would be like.

I could feel the sweat pouring down my face as they mocked me for thinking I would ever escape them, and they told me I thought I was so holy because people looked up to me. Their accusations were endless. I felt like I couldn't breathe, that they would snatch my life before the death chamber. I couldn't fight. They were too strong for me. Then it hit me! I knew the

One that was stronger than they were. I knew the One who had conquered them on the Cross. I knew Jesus!

As their strength seemed to grow and envelop me I began with all my might to say JESUS! The spirit of fear had a stranglehold on me but I whimpered over and over again, JESUS! I felt some relief, but I needed help so I cried out, "Jesus, help me!" That must have jarred my cellmate awake. He came leaping off of his cot and asked me what was wrong. He could see that I was struggling with an unseen force and later told me that he could feel something in the room and almost could not move off of his bed.

He immediately grabbed my hand and began to pray with me. This man prayed like I had never heard him pray before. He was authoritative and forceful as he began to bind up every demonic force in the room and cast them out in the name of Jesus. I heard him command the spirit of fear out of our cell and he asked for the peace and perfect love of the Holy Spirit to be released. He looked at me and could see the relief in my eyes. He just kept saying,

"Peace, peace, the peace of God. Jesus, we invite You into the room to surround us and we invite Your warring angels to war on our behalf."

And then: THEY WERE GONE!...for now.

I sat up and looked at the pool of sweat on my bed. He looked at me and said,

"Man, you got welts around your neck!"

I told him that I could not breathe and felt like my life was leaving me. He said that he had never encountered anything like that and he could feel a strong presence of fear in the room and it sounded like I was wrestling with something. I knew neither of us were going to get to sleep any time soon so we talked. We prayed. We read the Word and before we knew it we were singing praises to our God. He knew that the Holy Spirit had protected us and had fought for us. I said to him,

"Ty, I have never heard you pray like that." He said, "I felt the strength of God like never before. Something is changing in me for the better."

After that attack I knew it was time for me to face my enemy: fear. God was letting me know that, until I face them in His strength, they would continue to come. I sat down and I began to write. I started with my earliest memory of my tormentors. I wrote about how I would sometimes wake up with physical manifestations of an attack on my body. I wrote down how my dad would move us around from place to place like he was running from something or someone. Then I thought about the occult items that I found in the house. I remembered how, once I got here, I saw a demonic spirit wearing a black robe with the letter "S" written in red and how it seemed to pass through me. Finally I wrote down the dream about the old lady who I had since found out was my great, great, great grandmother and how she prayed for God to raise up someone in her generation to break the curse. BINGO! I had to study every Scripture on generational curses and then I needed to speak privately with Pastor Jonathan.

I knew I needed someone who was on a much higher spiritual level than I was to pray in agreement with me and to also cover me in prayer. I told him what was going on and what happened in my cell and that God was taking me on a fast. He told me that he and his prayer team would cover me and that he personally was going to fast with me. I had only gone on a fast one other time for spiritual growth but in Matthew 17:21 Jesus lets us know that there are some demons that will only leave by the combination of prayer and fasting. I had to seek God carefully in regard to the fast because when you live in a place like prison officers take notice if you are not eating for long periods of time and think you are trying to commit suicide. I did not want to draw any attention to myself so God led me to study the book of Daniel, particularly chapter 10. According to the Bible, Daniel did not eat any pleasant bread or flesh (meat) and he did not drink any wine.

Being in prison, our menu is chosen for us so I ate no meat or bread and because I have a horrible sweet tooth, I ate no sweets. Of course we do not get wine in prison so I gave up caffeine. I did this for 21 days and ended on the Esther's fast found in the book of Esther which is three days of no food or drink. Since God was leading me I knew the officers would not notice the last three days of the fast. I was serious about a strong move of God in my life, getting to know Him better and ending this curse that had plagued me and my family! There was also no way that I was willing to ever bring children into this world, God willing, and have them suffer the way I had. I got busy.

One after the other I looked up Scriptures that would help me: Exodus chapter 20 and chapter 34, Leviticus chapter 26, Numbers chapter 14, 1 Samuel chapter 15, 1 Samuel chapter 28, 2 Chronicles 33:6, the book of Esther, Proverbs 18:21, Ezekiel chapter 18, the book of Daniel, Matthew chapter 12, 2 Corinthians chapter 5, Galatians chapter 3 and chapter 5. I studied them carefully. I also studied Ephesians chapter 6, all of the book of James, and 1 John chapter 1. Pastor Jonathan taught us that we are no longer under the law of the Old Testament but under grace: however, the Old Testament is as important as the New Testament because not only does it point to Christ but it also gives us history.

I began the very next day. Each morning my cellmate and I prayed together then I would go off on my own. Ty told me he was fasting also and so were many of the brothers from our men's group. When Pastor Jonathan came in he said,

"The prayer team is busy keeping you surrounded in prayer. Hadassah felt a stirring also to intercede and fast with you."

Of course, that made me smile. I could feel the prayers helping me through this. I can also tell you this: the more I stayed before the Lord talking to Him and getting His Word in me the stronger I felt.

I prayed for days thanking God for His goodness and His mercy that He would allow His Son to die for me. I thanked Jesus for being willing to die and hang on a Cross for me. It literally took days to tell God just how appreciative I was of His greatness.

Then I looked deeply at myself. The first thing I thought was:

"Lord, I know that You love me but I can't even understand that. I was not even looking for You while I was in my sin. You came along when I needed You the most, in the woods that night when I was about to take my life and You stopped me."

Now I could see the filthiness of my own heart as I thought about the girls that I had been intimate with and prayed for forgiveness. I asked the Holy Spirit to untie every soul tie that had been created in my soul for being with those ladies. I repented one by one and asked that God would please save them if they had not come to know Him yet.

What surprised me mostly during my time of repentance was how willfully I prayed for the one who had murdered my friends. I felt passionate about asking God to draw him into His loving arms and forgive him. I cried and cried while on my knees telling God I forgive him. The words went from "Lord, please forgive him" to "I forgive you." I prayed that the Lord would have compassion on him and persuade him to come forward and admit to the crime, but I did not dwell on that. I was not going to make my time of prayer all about being released although I did pray about it and thank God for it.

I spoke and prayed Scriptures on truth over my situation because God does not function in lies. I knew the devil had me come here to kill me but God MET ME HERE and saved me. I prayed for the truth to be released, for me to be acquitted of this wrong, and thanked Him for doing this. I asked God to prepare me, my attorney and my family for my upcoming trial. I knew I needed to lay that at God's feet but it was also my reality. My prayer became,

"God, if they give me death, I will die in You. If I leave this prison, I will live for You. Either way, I win."

I didn't believe that the God that I served would let my life be taken for what someone else did.

When my father flashed before my face I felt a sadness. I knew that my dad had done his best for us and I had to understand that because he did not yet know Christ he did what he felt he should do. I also didn't understand his reasoning for telling my mom and brother not to write me, but because he is the head of the household, and they are both now Christians, they knew to honor his request. I prayed for God to save him and I asked God to forgive me also for being disrespectful to him and for every time I dishonored him. I stopped praying, got up and began to write my dad a letter asking his forgiveness and telling him how much I loved him. He had said that Mom and Brian were driving him nuts talking about Jesus so I figured rather than bombard him with more I needed to show him God by trying to be an example of Christ.

As I went through my time of repentance I asked God to show me my own heart. I wanted to see what was hiding that I didn't even know was there. Jeremiah 17:9 talks about how the heart is deceitful and asks,

"Who can know it?"

It goes on to explain that God searches the heart. God, our Creator, knows all about us so even though this organ is pumping inside our bodies we still need Him to reveal those hidden things. After I prayed for this, Kevin, the brother who punched me in the face, when I tried to break up the fight, walked past my cell. I felt a burst of anger! I thought I was over that incident because so much time had passed. It is certainly not true that time heals all wounds. Time can heal the physical wounds, but not the emotional. I had to go to him and get this straight, which I did. When I talked to him, he lowered his head and said,

"I didn't know how to approach you because I was so ashamed." I told him that I forgave him and he hugged me and thanked me. God is good, I'm telling you!!

The next part of my fast I spent praying and asking God to forgive my familial sins. There were many things that I had no part in, such as belonging to the occult, practicing witchcraft, and partaking in sacrifices, but because they were committed by my family, I repented on behalf of all of us. I renounced our sin-sick ways and called out everything that I knew we were guilty of. I asked the Holy Spirit to purify my bloodline and to not only break every curse but to utterly destroy every curse! All at once I felt the powers of hell coming against me. It was indeed my time to stand strong in the power of the Lord and to show them that I believe that "greater is He that is in me, than he that is in the world" (1John 4:4).

I reflected on Matthew 12 beginning at verse 43 where Jesus is teaching about unclean spirits: that when they go out of a man they go through dry places looking for another soul to torment. When they don't find a place where they want to stay they come back to that man and peer into his house (us) and see that we are empty, swept and clean. Having a clean house is a good thing but because that man has left his house empty the unclean spirit that was made to leave goes and gets seven more that are worse than it. They come back and torment the soul even worse than before. He says that the last state of that man is worse than the first! As I renounced my sins and the sins of my family I asked the Holy Spirit to go into each area and to occupy those territories. I didn't feel anything but I believed in faith. It's not about feeling emotions. It is knowing and believing that what we pray, and believe God for, is done. I knew that because I prayed according to His Word that it was being done. The darkness was being displaced by the light!

One evening God visited me so beautifully that I woke up thanking Him. I thanked Him because I knew that my prayers were being heard. When you know how insignificant you are you can't help but be in awe at how the God who framed all of creation would even take time to think about you. As I lay asleep, I began to dream. It was a beautiful day and the sun was shining bright. I was walking in a cemetery and there were people visiting graves of loved ones and placing flowers at their tombstones. As I continued walking I watched a man who was walking on the opposite side of the cemetery. He was dressed in what looked like a type of robe. It was blue and white, nothing fancy, and had some sort of a sash across the chest. As I watched Him, He watched me. When we were directly across from each other He walked briskly over to me. He had so much peace in His eyes and I felt that this was the Lord Jesus. He took a glass and poured what appeared to be oil over my head. He said,

"I am anointing you for your work."

I didn't see Him again after that.

When I woke up I had so much joy inside me. Did you ever have such a wonderful dream that you wish you could stay in it just a little while longer? That was how I felt. I wanted to just hang out with Jesus for a few more minutes and even ask Him,

"What work?"

I knew the answer was coming so I just laughed and said,

"Thank You Lord."

I thanked God for girding my loins with truth, covering my chest with the breastplate of righteousness, having my feet shod with the preparation of the gospel of peace, for the shield of faith and the helmet of salvation and the sword of the Spirit which is the Word of God, teaching me to pray always in the Spirit, and for watching with perseverance and supplication for all saints (found in Ephesians chapter 6)! I thanked Jesus for His blood that was shed for me. I continued to call on Jesus' name and for every demonic power to leave me, my atmosphere and family and for the light of God to fill us.

I knew Satan was defeated because my friend Jesus had defeated him. I ended my prayer with this:

"Dear lord, please always keep me clothed in Your humility."

When I rose up for the men's group later that day, I could feel the Spirit of God surrounding me. For the first time in my life the fear was gone. I knew that there would be times when the demonic would challenge me but I had a new confidence in Christ. I held in my heart the fact that Jesus had conquered Satan on the Cross and because Jesus abides in my heart, I could put Satan under my feet where he belongs! I had His Living Word on the inside of me and I had joy from being in His Word. I read and proclaimed it over my life, my family, my friends, people working in the prison, my trial, my release and even the one I was in prison for. When I woke up I started my day with the Word and dressed myself in the Armor of God. Before every meal I opened my Bible and gave thanks. Before I laid my head down to sleep, I read His Word. I just couldn't get enough!

When I came to the last three days of my fast I went back to thanking God and praising Him for just being God. It is difficult for the human mind to comprehend or even grasp the love of Christ. Rather than trying to understand it I just enjoyed it and thanked Him for loving me and not allowing me to die in my sin. I thanked Him for choosing me to be the one to stand against the devil on behalf of my family and I thanked Him for setting us free. I spoke and believed that every person related to me by blood on both sides would come to Christ because I believe that God died for every household, He has the power to save every household!

It is Finished

I was seeing my attorney more often as my court date approached. I was so thankful to have Pastor Jonathan and his church family and the men here in the prison praying for me. I felt God on every side. I knew that I needed as much prayer as possible to withstand this trial. I had hoped so much that my family would be there but I understood if they were not.

This was the last day of my fast and I occupied my time by reading the book of Nehemiah. I held onto his words in chapter 8 verse 10 that says,

> *"Then he said unto them, Go your way, eat the fat, and drink the sweet, and send portions unto them for whom nothing is prepared: for this day is holy unto our Lord: neither be ye sorry; for the joy of the Lord is your strength."*

WHEW WEE! That last part leaped into my heart. I went to Galatians 5: 22-23 and studied the fruit of the Spirit. I went back to the fruit of joy and I understood that because the Holy Spirit is eternal there is a difference between happiness and joy. Happiness comes and goes but joy is forever. It has no ending because the Holy Spirit has no ending. I told myself that I WILL walk in the joy of the Spirit no matter what!

I was surprised I had received a letter from my dad! I was actually nervous opening it and my hands shook. There were also letters from Mom, Brian and my Granddad. Dad's letter was the first that I read and as I went through it the tears fell from my face. He told me that he appreciated my words and that he has always forgiven me because I was his son. He asked me to forgive him for not being the father that he should have been. He then made such an honest confession to me. He told me that before he and my mom started having children he should have learned how to love. He said that he never felt loved by his father or really his mother and so he just didn't know how to express it to me or Brian other than by working hard and providing for us. He mentioned that he knew how tough it was to constantly be moved around but that was the only way he knew how to keep us safe, especially me. He ended his letter with this:

"You are my son and I know that you are innocent of this, so when you come home I would really love it if you would allow me to treat you to a father/son day. I remember how much you love baseball, so how about a game and maybe dinner?"

My heart was so overwhelmed! My dad was making an effort to start fresh and I couldn't wait to tell him that he was on! I had to just let his words soak in. He made no mention of Jesus but I continued to believe for him and thanked God for dealing with his heart and then, next, I read my moms' letter. Hers opened with a Scripture, Psalm 62:1:

> "Truly my soul waiteth upon God: from Him cometh my salvation."

This was the sweetest music. My mom was now a born-again Christian and I just felt her love with every single word.

She told me how much she missed me and that she couldn't wait to see me again and wrap her arms around me. She said that every day I had been taken from her made her appreciate those nights she lost sleep cuddling me, when I was a child, as she tried to comfort me. I could feel a hint of sadness but I knew that because she was now a follower of Christ that He would see her through this.

Brian's letter gave me special encouragement. He was about to graduate high school and said that although I couldn't be there he would make sure to send me a picture of him in his cap and gown. I loved this boy with everything in me and I was so proud of his accomplishments. He told me he was an honor roll student and was heading off to college to study medicine. He said that he believed God was leading him into this field to send him to countries that did not have much so that he could help where he was needed. I said,

"God, only You could help this boy get through school like this with all of the strain of this case."

Grandad's letter just said how much he loved me and in his special way,

"We're praying for ya Tiger!"

He was sometimes a man of few words but when he spoke, he spoke with love. I felt like I was at a family reunion even inside these walls. God let these letters get here just in time to encourage me. I tucked them under my pillow to keep them close and drifted off to sleep.

As I rested in God, I dreamed that I was on a ship surrounded by people. When I looked over to my right, there was the beautiful Hadassah. She was squatting next to a baby in a car seat and praying for the child. I went over and stood behind her and joined her in prayer. I looked up and saw an older child, probably about the age of five, walking in my direction.

For some reason I could not take my eyes off of him. As he passed me I saw a familiar hatred in his eyes as he glared at me. He opened his mouth as though to speak but it was the voice of a demon and he kept going. I was stricken with fear! Hadassah either didn't hear anything or just paid no mind to it.

I saw the child again as I was standing with what appeared to be ministers: don't ask me how I knew that. This time he said nothing but I was overcome with fear again. I wasn't afraid of the child but what was inside of him. I noticed a large man behind him. This time a demonic voice came out of this strong man and I backed away from him. When he had me against the wall of the ship he told me he was going to destroy me. I looked at him and said, "The blood of Jesus!" The strong man groaned and staggered back. I said it over and over again as this demon possessed man writhed in what seemed to be pain. With every step that he took backward I took a step forward until we were now on the opposite side of the ship and he was almost against the wall. I could feel my hands burning and this time I ran at him. I looked him in the eye and said with the authority of Christ, "I DESTROY YOU WITH THE BLOOD OF JESUS CHRIST!" I laid my hands on his chest and he let out the most tortured scream I've ever heard! It was so booming that it woke me up.

As I collected myself I heard God say,

"I have formed you as a weapon, fit for your work."

I knew that He was calling me to preach His word and that Hadassah would be by my side. There was nothing I could say but,

"Yes Lord."

And I rejoiced that He loved me so much that He would trust me to share the Gospel with His people. All I wanted to do was be obedient to Him and follow Him. He was my everything and I thanked Him for this tiny cell where so much growth had taken place. I prayed and asked that when I leave if He would allow whoever would take this cell after me to be filled with His Spirit and that it be a lifeline to Him.

Monday came and I felt very emotional because I didn't know if I would see these men ever again. I knew I was leaving to go back to where I had been arrested and face a jury of my peers. I felt a bit of a lift when I saw Pastor Jonathan and Hadassah. She was as beautiful as ever. I whispered to God:

"Please make me the husband that she needs, and help us to honor You throughout our time together."

I was surprised that I was praying this way. I was calling myself her husband. Hmm, who'd a thought?

Service opened and Brother Michael called me up front as Pastor Jonathan stood beside him and nodded his approval. I didn't know what this was about but I was obedient. Michael asked for all of the brothers and Hadassah to please extend their hands in my direction to pray for me and the upcoming trial. He looked over at Pastor Jonathan to pray but Pastor Jonathan told him to go for it. Michael prayed with a power that went through me. He commanded the truth to be revealed and I could hear the brothers praying in agreement with him. I felt like I was not going to be able to stand. God was pouring His strength into me and I could feel His anointing. My face and hands were on fire!

When he said "amen," Pastor Jonathan stepped forward.

"God has spoken to me about you from day one. You are like my son."

He floored me with his next words.

"When you leave the prison, come back to this city so that you can begin your training as a minister of the Gospel with me and my team."

I remember saying,

"JESUS!"

He told me to lift my hands, which I did. He laid his hand on my head. I could feel God pouring His strength and so much love into my heart that I could barely stand. The church erupted in praise!

When things quieted Pastor Jonathan asked me to address the group. He and Michael sat down. Hadassah wore a smile which made me melt. I looked around the room and knew to not waste time talking about my innocence or how I wanted the guilty party to be captured. Instead, I said,

"Had I not been allowed to come to this place I would still be out there running from God."

Everyone said "amen." I shared my story about how I had grown in God since being here and shared many of the Scriptures that had gotten me through. I encouraged them to,

"Continue to put God before yourselves. When you see a brother struggling or falling away take time to reach out to him. We are all connected and because God has changed our DNA we are now all family."

I could see tears falling from the faces of these grown men. I shared with them that in these days God is raising up people who will stand firm on His Word and will not mix the holy with the profane so never back down from His truth and never compromise. I told them that whether it is inside these walls or out on the streets, speak the Gospel in season and out of season and stand with a boldness for Jesus. I looked at each one of them and said,

"I love you with the love of Christ."

I ended it with a Scripture that I thought was very appropriate:

> *"Finally, brethren, farewell. Be perfect, be of good comfort, be of one mind, live in peace; and the God of love and peace shall be with you."* – 2 Corinthians 13:11.

I had truly come to love these brothers and respect them. As I looked around the room I could see clearly how God does not favor one person over another. Some of them are here for unimaginable crimes but prison was their breaking place and now they serve God with a passion. I can't wait to hear of the things that the Lord will use them to do.

I looked at Pastor Jonathan and told him that I did not know how long my trial would last or what the outcome was going to be but I would make my way back to him and his powerful ministry. I thanked him for being the father that I needed and the mentor that I did not deserve. I thanked him for coming into the prison and taking his time to teach the Word of God to people whom society sees as lost. I asked him if he would please thank the church and especially the prayer team for praying for me and that I would appreciate if they would continue to do so. With more tears in my eyes I ended with,

"Thank you for everything."

Then I briefly said to Hadassah, trying to hide my feelings,

"Thank you for praying for my situation, and I especially thank you for the powerful message you taught us about the kind of woman a Christian man should be looking and praying for. That message will always stay with me."

I didn't want us to be sad like we were at a funeral! I asked everyone to stand and said,

"Let's sing a praise unto our God."

And boy, oh boy, the celebration was in the air!

Service ended and we all hugged and tried to keep the tears from falling. You could tell that we were all so strongly connected that it was difficult to say goodbye, so we opted to say, "till we meet again." The officers came and called us pod by pod and we parted company.

Back in our cell Ty and I stayed up late talking and laughing. We had such a good time. I told him that he was always going to be my brother and that I would do everything I could to stay in touch with him. I certainly didn't want to lose a good friend. I hoped that one day we could meet up with each other on the outside. You just never know what the Lord has in store.

Wednesday morning I was ready to go. My few belongings were packed and searched and I was handcuffed and shackled. Me and some of the other inmates were ready for transport. I didn't know where they were going and I really didn't care. I had too much on my mind. The last time I was home the squad car I rode in was surrounded by an angry mob screaming obscenities and threatening to kill me. I felt very anxious and kept repeating to myself,

"Be anxious for nothing, Peter. God's got this."

Eventually I was able to take a short nap.

People think that God doesn't have a sense of humor but they're wrong. One of the officers involved in the transport was Officer Terrie. All I could do was enjoy the comedy. I didn't know what made this man so angry but he certainly was on my list of people to keep in prayer. Bless his heart! We were now about fifteen miles outside my destination. Officer Terrie turned around and the only thing he said to me the entire trip was, 'You look a might bit too fancy to be from around these parts." I just smiled and went back to looking out the window.

We entered town and I couldn't believe how things had changed in such a short time. The store where I used to work, Sal's, was now a café. I heard that Sal was living with his daughter now and had moved away. He sold the business since he didn't have the help he needed to keep up. I wondered how he was and just whispered,

"God please bless him wherever he is."

When we pulled up to the county jail, I was very relieved that there was no crowd, no mob, or reporters hanging around outside. I breathed easier. I was taken out of the transport van, escorted inside, and the officers did their Change of Custody to receive me. All of my belongings were searched again and I was handed over to the county jail Department of Corrections. They took me into a small room and as per the norm I was strip-searched to make sure that I wasn't trying to smuggle anything in, then was escorted to a single cell. They told me dinner would be in about an hour but I was too nervous to think about food. I needed spiritual food so I asked for my Bible. One of the officers returned with it and I thanked him. So far these officers didn't say much to me, but that was fine. I got into my Bible and prayed for Gods' presence to fill the atmosphere and asked Him to be with the ones who transported me here so that they got back safely.

My dinner came and was given to me through the slot and I sat it down. I just picked at it because nothing looked appetizing. I opened up the letters from my family and read their encouraging words again. It was just what I needed. I thought about all of the friends I had made at the other prison and prayed for them one by one. I kept my mind occupied with the things of God until it was time to sleep. Surprisingly, I rested well and even woke myself up a couple times snoring, which made me laugh.

The next day was preparation day for court and I would be meeting with my attorney to go over last minute details. When he arrived I was escorted to the attorney/client room where he waited for me. Attorney Maren was always difficult to read. When I walked in he looked very serious as he shuffled some papers around. He finally acknowledged me and sat back in his seat. He looked over his glasses at me and said,

"Well, I'm sure you know that I have been very busy preparing for your case and you haven't made this easy for me at all. So let me ask you this, are you ready to go home?"

I said,

"Well, I've been ready to go home sir."

He pulled his glasses off and said that this was one of the strangest cases he has ever overseen because of all of the twists and turns. He sat forward and said,

"Peter, do you know a Benjamin Jackson?"

I answered,

"I do, but where are you going with this?"

He said that late last night Mr. Jackson arrived at the police station with his father and a good attorney friend of mine, and confessed to both murders and even told the police where they could locate the gun that was used. It has been retrieved and the police are running forensics on it. He also told them that he acted alone.

Benjamin Jackson, AKA: Tank!

"I was good friends with him. I can't believe he would do this to Sam and Tony!"

Attorney Maren said,

"Well, believe it young man. You have just been acquitted of all charges and they are working on your release papers as we speak!"

He explained that Benjamin (Tank) had arrived at the field for our football game and expected everyone to be there but when he got there he saw that me and my brother weren't there. He said that he didn't know why he was in a rage but he went to the trunk of his car, grabbed the gun and as he approached the field he opened fire on Tony and Sam. He then placed the gun back in his trunk, drove to his aunts' house while she was out and hid it underneath the porch, deep in the back where no one would find it. Apparently, when he returned to the crime scene, I was there checking for signs of life and he heard me yelling for my brother and then saw me run away. He figured that since I was covered in their blood I would take the fall and he would be free to walk.

Everything was hitting me at once. I was a free man "almost" but Tank? The guy who hung out with us, partied with us and drove us around in his sports car all night looking for ladies to flirt with, he was the killer? Attorney Maren knew this would be hard for me to accept and told me that he had to go take care of some paperwork. The officers were going to take me back to my cell one last time so that I could pack. He said he had to wait for them to get everything done and that he had already called my parents with the good news and they were on their way. My dad had asked him to get me a fresh shirt, pants and shoes so that I could walk out of there as soon as I could. I gave him my sizes and said to just get something simple. I was trying to process all of this so clothes were the last thing on my mind. He said he'd return and the paperwork should be ready.

I was escorted back to my cell and collapsed by my bed. Tony and Sam's faces were flashing before me and I could only imagine the horror they must have felt seeing Tank raise a gun and slaughter them. I cried so hard. I was happy the truth had been told but also sad that I had walked so close to someone who was capable of this and let me be blamed for it! I asked God to help me because I could feel anger rising. I immediately began to intercede for Tank because I needed to be kept free from bitterness. I was heartbroken and, to be quite honest, I was just plain mad! I had been totally betrayed.

I had to deal with my feelings, not ignore them. I asked God,

"How could Tank have done something like that?"

God took me back to Ephesians 6:12 which says, that we do not wrestle against flesh and blood. Then something came back to me that I hadn't even thought of. One of Jesus' own disciples who walked with Him and witnessed countless miracles betrayed Him. In my humanity, I said to God,

"Yeah Lord but it was easy for You to forgive, You're God. It's built in You to forgive."

I heard the Lord say,

"That doesn't mean it did not hurt."

I knew this was going to take some time to get through but I was willing to go through it. The last thing I wanted was to carry around baggage that I was not meant to carry. Then God asked me,

"Peter, there was a time that you had absolutely forgiven this person before you knew who he was, why are you struggling with this? Can you not forgive those close to you who hurt and offend you?"

I said,

"God let Your will be done. I release him. Please fill me with Your love and let it flow through me for him. Father forgive me for puffing up and please forgive him because he didn't realize that he was being used by the devil."

I asked for God to save him and deliver him from evil.

I prayed for him until the officer came to my cell and asked me if I was ready to go. What a strange question! Of course I'm ready to leave this place. He escorted me to the front and gave me my belongings, which I signed for and then I turned to Attorney Maren who had a shopping bag for me. They let me step inside the restroom and change. It was a great pleasure to leave their department-issued jumpsuit inside!

When I came out Attorney Maren said that the police chief had held a press conference about 45 minutes ago to let everyone know the latest details in the case. He told the press that,

"Mr. Benjamin Jackson, along with his attorney, has come forward to confess to the murders of Tony Bryant and Sam Stokes and that the murder weapon has also been retrieved."

He ended it with,

"Peter Mason James has been acquitted of all charges and is now being released!"

When we stepped outside the jail there were reporters swarming the place. Microphones were being shoved in mine and my attorney's face for comment. I kept scanning the thick crowd for any sign of my family and then I spotted them. I made my way to them and we fell into each other's arms. I heard my mom weeping and my brother now towered over me, and he wept also. My dad kissed me on the cheek and said,

"It's finished son. Time to go home!"

The reporters still wanted a comment and once we were done embracing I clearly heard one of them ask how I felt to be cleared of all charges. I stopped and said,

"I am thankful to God for allowing the truth to come forward and now I am going to go and catch up with my family."

Another asked,

"Is it difficult to know that this was a friend of yours that let you take the blame?"

That question stung and I knew I still had more work to do in my heart but I managed to say,

"I am praying for Benjamin and his family."

Then I heard,

"Mr. James, what are your plans now that you have your life back?"

I smiled and said,

"Whatever God's will is. I'm going to take it one day at a time."

My attorney stepped in and told them that I was done answering questions as I was eager to be alone with my family.

They continued filming and taking pictures as we made our way to our vehicle. Attorney Maren's SUV was pulled directly behind it and we all shook hands. I thanked him for his work and for the clothes I was wearing. Mom told him that they were going to have a small welcome home party for me soon and would love for him and his team to come. He said to count him in and we all parted company.

I had never loved and appreciated my family more than that moment. Brian told me that graduation was in two weeks and he wanted me to help him shop for a suit. I told him I would be honored. Dad said, "Well don't forget that game I promised you," and smiled. Mom just reached in the back and held my hand and let the tears fall.

Before we got too far from the jail I asked Dad if he would pull over. He asked why and I told him that I wanted to give thanks to God. He said, "Sure." We all bowed our heads, including him, and I thanked God for everything I had experienced because it brought us to Him. I thanked Him for His love and kindness and for letting Tank come forward with the truth and asked if He would take care of him the same way He took care of me. I prayed for our safe travel home and thanked Him that I could lay my head down in my own bed tonight. We all said, "Amen."

The next few days were just full of love and hugs. Brian couldn't wait to introduce me to his love interest, a beautiful young woman named Anna, whom he met at church. I took my time trying to find my way around this new house. Dad certainly retired in style and there was room for half a football team! Mom busied herself doing something that I thought was strange. Although it was nowhere near Christmas, she pulled the Christmas tree out and said that it hadn't felt like they could celebrate without me so she was going to decorate and shower me with gifts for Christmas and my birthday from the last two years I missed.

It really made me laugh as we all stood around this Christmas tree, decorating it and singing Christmas songs. We had such a good time though! I couldn't ask for anything better. Mom had also been making plans for my welcome home party and had emailed everyone that she thought I would like to see. Granddad would be there along with a couple cousins who had helped mom through this. I also knew that Attorney Maren, his wife and legal team were attending.

The day of the party I walked around and took everything in. My family was here, the "holiday" decorations were up and the smells from the kitchen were driving me nuts! Mom had already smacked my hand for dipping my finger into her homemade cake frosting. The doorbell rang and people began to arrive. I was just so thankful to God and my loved ones! Dad welcomed everyone in as Brian took their jackets. We were all there, laughing and telling crazy jokes when the doorbell rang again. I looked around and wondered who it was since everyone was here and accounted for. I opened the door and found none other than Pastor Jonathan and his wife Isabella and standing behind them... Hadassah! My heart leaped!

Everyone was introduced and the Christmas decorations were explained to smiles and some chuckles. While everyone talked and visited with each other I asked Pastor Jonathan if I could see him privately. We went into the kitchen and Mom yelled,

"Peter, if I see any fingerprints in that frosting, I'm gonna get you!"

I said,

"Yes ma'am."

I closed the kitchen door and said,

"Pastor Jonathan... um, well about Hadassah, ah, would it be okay with you if I asked her out to lunch tomorrow?"

Since they lived several hours away they had reservations at a hotel.

He smiled at me and said,

"Peter, I think that would be just fine with me but what do you think she will say?"

And he giggled. He said,

"You know what, wait here and I'll go get her."

I think I was sweating clean through my shirt and I kept wiping my hands on my pants. I was actually shaking I was so nervous. She came in and said,

"Papa told me you wanted to see me."

This was NOT a good time for my tongue to be tied. I finally was able to get out,

"I was wondering if you would do me the honor of going to lunch with me tomorrow."

It seemed like an eternity before she answered. She said that she would like that very much. (Was I dreaming and if so, please don't wake me?!) She told me what hotel they were staying at and I asked her if 11:30 was okay? She smiled and said,

"Yes."

We returned to the crowd and I think both of us were wearing our feelings on our sleeves because almost everyone noticed. Granddad looked at me and said,

"She sure is pretty, my boy. You treat her like a lady or you will have to deal with me. I can tell that one is special."

I said,

"She sure is."

Before the end of the evening Hadassah and I took a walk around the property. We talked like old friends. She had the most amazing laugh I had ever heard.

There was a bench and a small pond behind the house and we sat down. She wanted to know how I was handling everything. I kind of poured my heart out to her and admitted that there were times when I got angry and then there were times that I was overwhelmed with sadness. I told her that I had never really had a chance to mourn my friends' deaths and now I was mourning another loss. She listened without judgment and when I was done talking I told her we should get back to the house.

As everyone was leaving and letting me know how glad they were I was home all I could think about was Hadassah and how honored I was that God had placed her in my life. I couldn't wait for tomorrow to come but I had no choice but to be patient.

The next day Dad loaned me his SUV, programmed the GPS to the location of the hotel, and handed me quite a bit of money. I thanked him. My dad still had not made a confession for Christ but he was a different man. This experience had changed him and he was learning how to show his love for his family. Granddad winked at me and warned me about what he said last night and then said,

"I pray the good Lord allows me enough time on this earth to see my grandsons married and my first great-grandchildren."

I said,

"Granddad, you'll probably outlive us all, but please slow down."

And we all laughed.

On my way to the hotel I picked up some flowers for her and for her mom. I also got a box of chocolates for Hadassah and then I was off. I felt like I was in a dream. My life had been so different just weeks ago. She last saw me in prison garb and now I am picking her up for lunch! When I got to the parking lot, I called her cell phone so that she knew I was there and I asked if her parents could meet me in the lobby also.

I walked inside with all of my gifts for the ladies and waited for the elevator doors to open. About three minutes later, there they were. I greeted everyone and handed the flowers to her mom and the other flowers and candy to Hadassah. As beautiful as the flowers were, they couldn't compare to her. She thanked me, gave everything to her dad, and said we wouldn't be out late, and we left. I opened the door of the vehicle for her, hopped in myself and we were off.

Dad had told me about a really nice Italian restaurant not far from the hotel. Hadassah said she loved Italian food so that's where we went. As we sat across from each other it was really something to finally be able to do this. I realized that we take so much in this life for granted and I wanted to savor every second. We talked and ate, laughed and talked some more. We were there so long that we actually ordered more food and before we knew it, it was 5pm.

I paid the bill and she spotted a mini mall across the road so we walked over to it and did a little shopping. I loved that her eyes lit up at the simplest things. She picked out a scarf and pair of earrings. I asked if I could buy them for her and we left for the hotel. I hated for our time together to end especially since they were heading back home the next day. As we entered the hotel, she called Pastor Jonathan to let him know that we were sitting in the lobby having coffee and after about 45 minutes I walked her to the elevator. She thanked me for the gifts and the wonderful dinner and good company. As the door to the elevator opened she said,

"Let's do this again, Peter Mason James."

I told her I would be honored. The elevator doors closed and I let out a sigh. I was in love and there was no denying it!

Over time, Hadassah and I got very close and we honored the Lord in our relationship. There was no way I wanted to blow this by being dumb and letting my hormones take over. When we weren't together we were on the phone or texting. I landed a pretty good job and was able to get a small car so I did the traveling to see her. She was worth it! We also made time to make sure that we spent time with the Lord as a couple. We studied the Word of God together and we loved to pray together. Everyone knew that she was "the one" and eagerly waited for me to pop the question. I chose my timing perfectly.

Closure

With all of the good and positive things going on in my life I felt like something was missing. I talked to Mom about this and just like the mother she is she said to me,

"Sweetheart, you need closure before you can move on."

That was exactly it! I needed to say goodbye to my friends and just let this out once and for all. I asked her and Dad if they would go back with me to where this all began so that I could visit their graves and say goodbye.

The next day we were on the road and the closer we got to our former home the more quiet everyone became. Dad finally just put the radio on to fill the silence. We pulled up at the cemetery and got out. They let me go ahead. I found Tony's site first and laid a small Cross at it. I spoke to him like he was standing there and told him how much I loved him and would never forget him. I then found Sam's grave and did the same thing. I asked God to bury my pain there so that I could release them and go on with life. It was very emotional but this was necessary. I felt Dad come up behind me and place his hand on my shoulder. We turned and joined Mom who was sitting in the SUV wiping tears from her face.

I climbed in and set my head back. I felt a peace within me but I still missed them. I guess when our loved ones leave us, we always carry part of them in our hearts. I thought about how we would run so hard playing football and how Tony and I always challenged each other at work to see who could lift the most. I was able to crack a bit of a smile as we drove away.

We got back on the highway and about three exits later Dad got off and Mom asked him why he was getting off at this exit. He said,

"We're going to get some ice cream."

She looked at me and I smiled. She looked back at him and said,

"You know what, Frankie? I sure do love you."

Dad glanced at her and said,

"You know what Kay? I love you back."

Then he looked at me in the mirror and said,

"I love my sons too!"

I was too choked up to say anything and he understood. I had never seen this side of him before.

We got home about midnight and everyone went to bed. Brian was off to college and he sent me a text that said,

"Bro you need to come and visit before you make any moves because I connected with a men's Bible study group that wants to hear your story."

I texted him back and told him to let me know when so I could clear it with my boss. He wrote back "YES!" This would be the beginning of doors that God would open for me. Before I knew it I was being asked to speak at detention centers and churches. I shared as God led me and I always allowed myself to be very honest about my experience, including the fact that I still sometimes struggled with unforgiveness for Benjamin. I tell people wherever I go that there is no sense in trying to hide your feelings from God because He knows what we're dealing with.

Hadassah and I had been dating for over a year and she was preparing to graduate college with her Masters Degree. Beauty and brains! She already had a job offer back home at a women's shelter and was eager to begin. Pastor Jonathan was happy to have his baby girl home, especially since her older sister had recently married and moved away and the middle girl accepted a job offer halfway around the world. I was so happy for Hadassah. She had worked hard and stayed on the Dean's List. God had truly blessed me.

My parents and I made arrangements for her graduation and we met up with her family. It seemed as if everyone had roses for her and all kinds of gifts. I decided to do something a little different and I bought her a necklace with pink (her favorite color) stones and a heart inside of a heart. She had captured my heart and this was my way of showing her.

Her family had plans for a huge party when her graduation was over. We slipped out the front door, as the party got on the way, onto the porch and I gave her the gift that my mom had so beautifully wrapped. She opened it and her eyes lit up! She jumped in my arms and said,

"I love you so much!"

We had said the "L" word to each other before but this was different. I held her in my arms and then pulled away, turned her around and placed the necklace around her neck. I told her that when I saw it I thought it was perfect because the hearts are interconnected and cannot be separated. I turned her back to me and said,

"Hadassah, my heart is yours."

She said she felt the same and we embraced. Her oldest sister opened the door and said that everyone was waiting for her to cut the cake. She ran over to her and said,

"Look what Peter gave me! Isn't it gorgeous?"

She showed it to everyone in the house. If I could have handed her the world, I would have done just that.

A couple of months later Hadassah made plans to come visit me because I had been asked to speak to a group and she wanted to support me. I had been working a lot of overtime to put money away and Dad was so gracious to let me stay home so I could do so. Everything had to be perfect for this visit. I had already talked to her parents about marrying her and they were beaming with joy so my plan was in motion.

She arrived and I picked her up from the hotel and we went to the church. We were greeted very warmly and I was excited. She noticed this so I tried to tone it down so I wouldn't give anything away. When service was over and we talked to everyone I told her that I was hungry and wanted to take her to a place I found. It was almost dark so it was perfect. I sent a text that we were on our way and asked her if she would humor me by wearing a blindfold. We drove for about a half-hour to a very secluded area that overlooked a beach. When I parked, she took the blindfold off and was a little taken aback that it was pitch dark. She asked where we were and I said,

"You'll see."

She said,

"Peter, I don't see any restaurant."

I told her to just trust me.

She took me by the arm and we walked into the darkness when all of a sudden we took a step and soft white lights began to turn on. With every step, as we approached the top of the hill, there were lights. When we got to the top, there was a table set for two and what she didn't see was that well off to the side there was a cart area where a chef and a waiter had been waiting for us. I pulled her seat out for her. The waiter came over to light our candles and tell us what was on the menu for the night. I had all her favorites prepared and he started with appetizers. Once he walked away the sound of a violin filled the air and the violinist came over to serenade us.

She was overwhelmed with what she saw but the night wasn't done. You could hear the waves crashing and smell the beach but you couldn't see it. When we were finished eating I asked her if she would join me for a walk. Again, with each step, soft white lights turned on as we walked down the steps on the other side of the hill and made it to the beach. The area began to light up so that she could see the water and I could see her beauty. You could still hear the violin and I told her how much she meant to me. I said,

"You have filled my life with the most beautiful colors and have added more and more to me. Knowing you has allowed me to experience the closest thing to God's joy in this earth."

I got down on one knee and said,

"Hadassah, if you will become my wife, I promise you that I will always hide your heart in mine, never to be separated. Will you marry me?"

I presented her with a ring. Through her tears she managed to give me a "yes" and dropped down to her knees. She threw her arms around me and said,

"Peter, I've known it was you since the day we met. I would love to be your wife!"

I placed the ring on her finger and we just sat in each other's arms and listened to the violin and the waves.

All of a sudden my phone went off and when I opened it, it was a text from her dad. The text said,

"Soooooooooooo?"

I told her it was him and showed her the message. She called him and put him on speaker phone and said,

"Daddy, I'm getting married!"

He said,

"Baby Girl, your mother and I are so happy that she can't even talk right now."

Hadassah said,

"Tell her that we have a wedding to plan."

I called my parents who were waiting by the phone and told them and Hadassah heard a yell from their end. I put it on speaker and I could tell that Mom was crying. Dad told her,

"Welcome to our family."

Granddad yelled,

"It's about time!"

We all laughed. I told them I wanted to call Brian and share the news with him and ask him to be my best man. They were so happy for us. When I called Brian and told him that Hadassah said yes, he said,

"Bro that is so awesome!"

Then he said something that really made Hadassah and I think and be very grateful. He said,

"Bro, do you realize that with everything you went through, if you hadn't experienced that, you two never would have met?"

It really is true that God can take something that is horrible and turn it around for our good and for His glory. When we were done reflecting on that, I asked Brian,

"Hey if you're not too busy with college and all, would you be my best man?"

He said,

"Bro, I would be honored."

The wedding plans were in motion. Pastor Jonathan insisted on paying for everything. He told Hadassah that her wedding was to be whatever we planned and the ladies, including my mom, got busy.

I Do and I Forgive

The wedding could not have been any better. Both families came together to celebrate and Hadassah decided to keep it small but it was elegant nonetheless. It was truly the second happiest day of my life. The first was meeting Jesus. We included Him at every turn because He was the reason for this union. The church was decorated beautifully and everyone had a hand in it. Everyone wanted to be a blessing to us, and they were.

The reception was held at her aunt's restaurant which she closed down for us. I splurged on a horse drawn carriage for my new bride and we enjoyed the warmth of the day as people on the street waved to us and yelled,

"CONGRATULATIONS!"

We returned the wave and yelled back,

"THANK YOU!"

When we made it to the reception I heard the DJ announce,

"Ladies and gentlemen, please welcome for the first time, MR. AND MRS. PETER MASON JAMES!"

The place erupted in cheers but I didn't hear a thing. All I could see was my beautiful Hadassah. In case you haven't figured it out yet, I love that woman!

My parents also blessed us by paying for our honeymoon in Hawaii. I cannot stress enough to you the importance of marrying the one who completes you. If you are a Christian, why not let God give you the best that He has for you? I could not imagine going through life tied to the wrong spouse. Also, waiting until you are married to become one with the person whom you adore is better than anything you can ever dream of. Our foundation was solid because we kept God first, front and center.

God continued to open doors for me with an amazing job at a home for boys. I could now help the young ones before they were in danger of going where I've been. Hadassah and I both had jobs we loved and we also joined her dad helping in his ministry. I loved being able to go back to the prison where this all started and see my brothers. I love those men so much. We were able to move into a small townhouse up the road from her parents and life was good.

Before we married we talked about starting a family as soon as possible so it wasn't long before I came home from work and she announced she was pregnant! A loving wife, good jobs and now this? God is so amazing! She made an appointment and we found out she was two months along and everything was going just fine. We both whispered "Thank You, Jesus." Eventually we found out that we were having a boy and after careful consideration we decided to name him Ezra, which means "help" or "helper." We enjoyed this pregnancy and even while he was in the womb we read the Word of God to him and sang Godly songs to him.

When Ezra Mason James came into this world the first thing I did was dedicate him to the Lord. I spoke that he would have peace in his life and that he would begin to follow Christ from an early age. I asked God to use him for His glory all the days of his life. After walking with God for some time and studying the Old Testament Scriptures I began to see that fathers in that time took the names of their children seriously and gave them names that were meaningful. They also would speak the blessings of God into their children's lives when they were born. He was our blessing and we cherished him.

God Moves in Mysterious Ways

Our son was three years old when we found out we were expecting again, this time, a girl. I asked Hadassah if she would mind if her first name was Hannah because my great, great, great grandmother had sent forth prayers that had been honored by God and that was her name. When we told Ezra that he was going to have a little sister and that the baby was growing in his mom's belly he politely placed his hand on Hadassah's stomach and told us he wanted to pray for her. We smiled and bowed our heads and I thought, well, this should be interesting to hear what is in a three-year-old's mind. His prayer was simple:

> *"Thank You God for my mommy and daddy and for my baby sister. Please let her grow good and have fun. And Lord please don't ever let her have more ice cream than me! Amen."*

I can't tell you how we laughed! My son ADORES ice cream. We said "amen" and I kissed him on the cheek. Although his prayer was simple and comical I thanked God that we were rubbing off on him. We pray with him every morning and every night before he goes to sleep and we make sure to read the Bible to him.

One day I walked into the house after work. Hadassah was busy at the stove cooking. Ezra was at the table coloring and we also had a dog named Charlie who was begging Hadassah for scraps. I greeted everyone and shuffled through the mail. I got to a letter that stopped me in my tracks and I had to sit down. Hadassah saw my reaction and asked who the letter was from. I said,

"Benjamin."

The only thing I could do was stare at it because it seemed like time had just stopped. She asked me if I wanted her to open it and I handed it to her. She looked at Ezra and asked him if he would go play in his room for a few minutes and he and Charlie took off.

She sat down across from me and carefully opened the letter. I didn't know what to expect but I certainly wasn't expecting this. I didn't know how I even felt but I had done a lot of praying for this man and now it was time to see what is truly in my heart! She unfolded it and began:

Dear Peter,

I know that I am the last person you ever thought you would hear from. I asked my dad to track you down because it was time for me to face you. I cannot begin to express my sorrow for what I have done to our friends, our families and especially to you. I want to first explain that night as best I can. Pete, there were times when it was everything I could do to keep it together. I felt like I had so much pressure on me to live up to what everybody thought I was. I was captain of the football team in high school, the big body builder in the gym, the perfect son to my dad, a ladies man to all the girls and the so-called cool one to my friends. Deep down inside I always felt like I was nothing. To be honest with you I worked so hard in the gym and spent so much time there because I didn't have to deal with my own reality.

I know you heard the rumors that I used steroids and those rumors were true. Those things sent me into rages but people thought it was all part of my bad boy image. There were so many times I felt like I wasn't even myself, like there was something taking over my mind. Most times I couldn't even sleep so I would work out even at home. I was losing my grip on reality.

The night of the murders, Pete, there was a darkness brewing inside of me like I had never felt before. I grabbed my dad's gun and loaded it in the trunk of my car and I set out on a mission. Now, this is hard for me to say to you but I need to, I was planning on killing all of you. Anyone that showed up that night was going to die at my hands and then my plan was to kill myself. I just felt so much hatred toward myself but I wanted to take it out on all of you first. I didn't care who was there, male or female, friend or stranger, they were going to die.

After I shot Sam and Tony I hid and waited for the rest of you but when you came and I saw you trying to help them I didn't want to kill you or myself. I decided to let you be blamed. I saw the blood all over you and I knew you would have some explaining to do so I disappeared and hid the gun. When I came back all of the police and ambulances were there and I saw them place you under arrest. I could have stepped forward then but I didn't. Instead I put on an act so that the police would have no reason to look at me.

Hadassah paused and looked at me. She could tell that my blood was boiling. I didn't even realize I was rocking back and forth in my chair. My hands were balled into fists. She took my hand and said,

"Release the anger, Peter. Don't go backward because God has brought you too far."

I stood up and walked over to the sink. She came behind me and placed her hand on my back. I took a deep breath and with tears said,

"God, I forgive him. Lord, You have forgiven me for so much and I forgive him. I will not allow the enemy into this household and I will not give him an inch of my heart! My heart belongs to You Lord. I forgive him."

I took another deep breath, turned around and I hugged my wife. I was so thankful she was there for me. She walked out to check on Ezra and I went back over to the letter.

It continued:

Pete, I know you may not ever forgive me for what I have done to you but I want you to know that I am sorry. I had to do this and come clean because God wanted me to.

Did he just say God wanted him to? I rubbed my eyes and read the line again then went on reading:

I know that often people come to prison and they all of a sudden find Jesus but believe me when I tell you, I have run long as I can. I finally surrendered to Him and I am still learning but I felt that now was the time to confess to you. I got tired of banging my head against the wall and living in torment every day. God is teaching me about His peace and I love the men's ministry here.

I have never experienced anything like this in my life. Every day that I wake up I have the realization that I deserve death and judgment but God saw fit to save me and love me. How does He love us even at our ugliest?

Well, I think I have left you with enough to chew on and again, Pete, I am so sorry. I can't tell you enough how I carry you and their families in my heart. I still have to write to them and apologize but I am letting God lead me first. I don't want to send a letter at the wrong time and upset them anymore than I already have. You may wonder how I knew it was time to send this to you. Well, the truth is, I wrote it a couple of months ago but I never felt like it was time. My cellmate, who is a great guy, talks to me a lot about God and the Word and he said that God would speak to my heart when it was time. He has taught me so much. As a matter of fact, you two know each other: Gabe. He told me to tell you hello.

I looked up to heaven and laughed and laughed. I mean, I laughed so hard that I had tears streaming down my face. Hadassah came back in and asked what was so funny and I just shook my head. I thought, this can't be Gabe from when I was in prison but I have never met another Gabe. I continued reading:

Pete, I am learning so much from this guy but it's so funny because he is always sitting at our little desk writing something. Every time I go to talk to him he is busy writing (letters I guess.) Oh, well. I told him I would be sure to tell you what he said. He told me that he won't be here much longer. I sure am gonna miss him when he leaves.

Again I was laughing. I don't know what to make of this man who has connected with Benjamin and I but he certainly works for God. I said,

"Lord, You have a way about You to get Your messages to those that You love, don't You?"

I sat quietly and thought about that explosion of anger that I had felt just minutes before and how now every drop of it was gone. All I could do was thank this great and mighty God who has allowed someone like me to be part of His family. I thought to myself how God used a prison to meet with me and now He is doing the same for Benjamin. I also noticed that he ended his letter with "BENJAMIN." That made me smile also because he is no longer "TANK."

Hadassah was just finishing dinner. I walked up to her, told her how much I love her, and grabbed the letter. I then went into Ezra's room and played with him for a bit. I told him that it was almost time for dinner and asked him to go into the kitchen and see if mommy needed help and like lightning he and Charlie were gone. I just love that little boy so much.

I went into the den, sat at the desk and searched for some paper. How could I not write my brother back and tell him how I have already forgiven him? I had an excitement brewing in my heart and even hoped that one day I could go visit him. I thanked God for hearing all of our prayers and thought about all of my blessings. My mom and brother were saved. Brian is on the Dean's List in school and engaged to his wonderful girlfriend. Dad had still not committed to Christ but he was a changed man and well on his way. Granddad was full of the wisdom of God and also full of humor. He is such a delight to be around when I go see my folks. You already know how I feel about my Hadassah. We are growing together each day and serving God in ministry alongside her dad who I am thankful to still call my mentor. Life is good and God is better! I grabbed my pen and began to write:

My Brother In The Lord, Benjamin…

Grateful Heart

I want to thank you if you are still reading my story. I hope that my words have left you encouraged to understand that you are not crazy and you are not alone if you have been through what I've been through spiritually. When I decided to put my story on paper it was never with the intention of becoming famous or rich. All I wanted to do was help someone. I wanted to share what Jesus has done in my life with others. My prayer is not that you were entertained, but awakened!

I pray that by the time you got to the last line of my story that you were well aware of Jesus' love for you. It doesn't matter what you have done, where you live, how much money you do or do not have in the bank. He died for all of us! What a wonderful thing to know that as the world becomes more chaotic, we who belong to Christ can walk in His peace, His blessing, His victory and His love. I would encourage you that after you meet Christ, pass His love along. If you already know Him, pass His love along.

For those who feel discouraged, YOU CAN MAKE IT! Look up to God and let His love wash over you. YOU CAN MAKE IT!!

Lastly, I want to share just one more dream with you and I hope this will help those in ministry. In the dream, God took me to a highway. I watched the cars driving in every direction. I began to run on the highway and the Holy Spirit lifted me over it. I opened my mouth and I heard the blast of what sounded like a trumpet. Then I heard the Fathers voice and it was not a gentle, loving voice. He said,

"My people are always running here and there and saying that it is I who is sending them but I have sent them nowhere."

He compared their seeking fame and fortune to lasciviousness and He was not pleased.

I get invitations to many places to tell my experience but before I say to them that I will be there I tell them I need to pray about it first. I have realized that sometimes a door that is being opened, even for ministry purposes, is not always being opened by God. How can we go and share a message with people, if we don't know that God is sending us? Don't allow yourself to become so busy with "kingdom work" that you forget about the "King of the kingdom." We must also not seek after wealth and fame because when they become god, we lose sight of God. He must be first in our lives. He must order our steps.

Hadassah and I have made sure to keep God first with prayer, Bible study, fasting and obedience. Does this mean that we are perfect? Absolutely not! However, I believe this is key to being a successful Christian:

> *"But seek ye first the kingdom of God, and his righteousness; and all these things shall be added unto you."*— Matthew 6:33

— Peter Mason James

Word from the Author

I began writing this in September of 2011 after seeing part of it in a dream. The Lord woke me up and said,

"Write it down so that you do not forget it."

I did so and peacefully drifted off to sleep again. Because I was instructed to write it down, I knew there was something to it. I took the one scene that I saw in the dream and prayed about it. From there, God began to give me what to write around it. I wrote the first five chapters and then it happened: I went blank! I put it away for years until I met with a talented young man named Seann, who is very gifted in the area of film and music. He looked at me and said,

"I know why you stopped writing: FEAR."

Well, he was right. I was afraid of putting myself out there on this level. I began praying against the spirit of fear, grabbed my laptop, sat down, and once again began to write. God poured this through me and every time I read it, I cry. That's how I know it came from Him. I am so honored that He has trusted me with this and I pray that it helps you with any of your struggles you are facing. Remember these few things: Nothing is too hard for the Lord, Everything that gets to you has to go through His hands first, and whatever struggle you face, Jesus already defeated it on the Cross!

BECAUSE HE DEFEATED IT, YOU HAVE THE VICTORY!

Much Love,

Simply, Me

On Tuesday December 5, 2017 I had a dream that I would like to share with you. I was outside at work and scolding these boys that I caught doing something dangerous. Once the scolding was over, I chatted with these brothers as they were identical twins and we had a very pleasant conversation. As we spoke, I looked up and the clouds parted. I looked at them and told them,

"Please confess Jesus as your Savior and do it now!"

I could hear people behind me that had seen the clouds parting excitedly saying,

"It's Jesus! Jesus is coming back!"

We were gone in an instant, flying through the clouds to meet our Savior in the sky. All I could feel was joy as every person sang the same song of praise in one accord. I looked to my left and there was our Savior. Jesus was in the midst of us and I began to say,

"My Jesus! You're with us!"

The love was almost overwhelming.

I believe God wanted this dream to be part of this book because He is coming back for His church, those who have confessed Him as Savior and believe God raised Him from the dead, according to Romans 10:9. This is a promise He made to us in His Word. No one knows when He will come, but He is coming....

WILL YOU BE READY?

www.ingramcontent.com/pod-product-compliance
Lightning Source LLC
LaVergne TN
LVHW051551070426
835507LV00021B/2525